I THINK IT'S FUNNY ...

Tom O'Daniel

ARCHWAY PUBLISHING

Archway Publishing books may be ordered through booksellers or by contacting:

Archway Publishing
1663 Liberty Drive
Bloomington, IN 47403
www.archwaypublishing.com
1 (888) 242-5904

ISBN: 978-1-4808-9200-2 (sc)
ISBN: 978-1-4808-9201-9 (e)

Library of Congress Control Number: 2020912042

Print information available on the last page.

Archway Publishing rev. date: 08/27/2020

CONTENTS

FOREWORD

In the handful of books I have read the forwards have something in common – they are generally boring. First are the "thank you" s to people for contributing in some manner. A few that should have been mentioned are probably left out, causing some heartburn. I am sure to do the same.

Next, reference material is listed - books that have great meaning with underlying messages giving the impression of deep meaning to come. My resource material is Webster's Dictionary, spellcheck, Jeff Foxworthy's book "No Shirt, No Shoes, No Problem", and Lewis Grizzard's book "Elvis Is Dead and I Don't Feel So Good Myself."

The stories are from my memory, with a few contributed by friends.

As you enter a book store, you see many categories. There are shelves with books on finance, management, sex, religion, fiction ... the list is endless. This book has stories of four types. The first category includes true stories. The second category is slightly modified because of poor memory. The third category is slightly modified to make them funny. The fourth category is outright lies, mostly from my friends.

My first thank you goes to an English teacher at Dunbar High School in Dunbar, West Virginia. This lady did not spend much time combing her hair, putting on makeup or brushing her teeth. We called her Death Breath. My attitude and conduct in her class were far from stellar, and any time I even considered doing something wrong she was in my face. She twisted an ear and called me impertinent. I didn't even know what that meant but the look on her face said it had to be bad. And the breath … oh! She moved me directly in front of her desk where we were eyeball to eyeball. It was more than I could take, so to myself I said, "You win!" I made the decision to get an A in the class, and to her surprise, I did. Years later, I became an office manager in Norfolk, Virginia. I was able to write a business letter, and even correct letters done by the office staff. Mrs. Summerfield came to mind, and the fact that she taught me to spell, punctuate, and all of the basics to be proficient in an office. Thank you, Mrs. Summerfield, for taking the time to turn around a goof-off. I apologize for my bad attitude and poor conduct.

I would like to thank Bill Stephens, a lifelong friend and co-conspirator in many funny situations. There was no time when anything to get of laugh was out of bounds. As an example of our conduct, a business associate and I had traveled to Manassas, Virginia, looking for an additional location for a store. Bill was my corporate attorney and had arranged to meet us with a real estate agent at the prospective location. As I was walking beside the agent, Bill (my attorney) was trying to hook my foot from behind to make me stumble and fall beside the attractive lady real estate agent. Thanks Bill.

My Dad was the source of many wacky situations and certainly an influence. Norman Baker, who, after hearing an illogical statement by a fellow historian, began research and writing. Norman has written several successful books refuting that illogical statement. My daughter, Gwyn (O'Daniel) Bell, who converted my left-handed scribble to readable text. To all my friends whose laughter gave me the impression that this could sell. The stories were told in the evening, in a pleasant setting that included adult beverages being served, setting the proper atmosphere. When attempting to write these stories at 6:30 in the morning it just wasn't funny. Therefore, it is highly advised to start with the proper setting and a favorite beverage before indulging in this book.

Some of the stories to be included in this book are of real people in my life and are less than flattering. I asked a friend who is an author and another who is an attorney if mentioning their names could cause possible legal action against me. The answer was that if the stories were considered derogatory it was possible. They asked if any could be taken in that manner and my answer was about half of them. Looking back on my life, for some reason the funny incidents and stories stand out. I remember anything funny. Could be a defense mechanism, as there were a number of bad events, but I choose not to think about those. In making the decision to write a book the first question was, “Do I have a sufficient number of stories to fill a book?” I purchased an 8 ½ x 11 notebook and placed it on a table to list potential stores. Within a few minutes there were three columns from top to bottom of potential stories, so here we go!

MY DAD

My Dad is where I'll start, as watching him and many of the wacky things he did molded me into whatever I am now. In watching him, I would try to incorporate the good and avoid the things that were negative.

My Dad was heavily influenced by the depression era and as far as he was concerned we were still in it. This mindset determined most everything in his life, including clothing, car, fishing, hunting, and business.

During World War II he drove a newspaper delivery truck for the Charleston Gazette on a route that went from Charleston to Point Pleasant on the Ohio River. The roads were narrow, and the papers were passed before daybreak. Often, he would see a rabbit sitting in the road. He would run over the rabbit, hitting it in the head with the bumper, and we had road kill for the table. Rationing during World War II made this an important item. I have a meat ration slip for me saying I was malnourished during the war.

A neighbor of Dad's worked in the garage where the papers were picked up for delivery. He said that all the guys in the garage looked forward to Dad coming in so they could hear what he had to say. A supervisor asked Dad about the number of papers he was delivering when he returned one day. The reason for this was to determine if there were more papers than subscriptions, allowing Dad to keep the full amount of money. His answer was, "On a clear day I don't have enough and on a foggy day I have too many."

Dad, my brother Joe, and several others went deer hunting near Brandywine, West Virginia. We were there over a weekend and were seeing no deer. We were using shotguns with pumpkin balls, as having a rifle would cost more money. The first shell loaded was a shotgun shell with pellets, as there were a few rabbits and squirrels. If a deer came along we could eject the shotgun shell, leaving the pumpkin ball. Dad's buddy, Raymond Barnette, was sitting on a log with his 30.30 lever action on his lap. A grouse started drumming on the other end of the log. Raymond knew that raising his rifle to aim would have the grouse on the fly and difficult to hit. His rifle was pointed in that direction, so he fired from his lap. The slug took the head off the grouse. Dad was nearby in the woods and came over to see what Raymond was shooting at. They both laughed and couldn't believe the luck of a shot from the lap. Raymond asked Dad if he would take the grouse in the game pouch on the back of his hunting jacket, and of course he did. A little later

Dad was walking along with a local farmer and they jumped another grouse. Grouse are very difficult to kill because they scare you as they jump and fly. In addition, they fly low, changing direction as they go. Dad leaned forward, aimed and fired, killing the grouse. He hadn't killed a grouse in years and was amazed he even hit it. As he went over to pick up the grouse, the farmer started saying how amazing the shot was, killing a flying grouse with a pumpkin ball. When Dad returned to the farmer, he reached into the other side of the pouch, pulled out Raymond's grouse, and said, "Yeah, I just shot his head off." For the next two days the farmer was bringing people by to see the grouse and telling them about Dad's shot. Dad just played the role.

Dad began selling cash registers and office machines in the coal fields and small towns of West Virginia. In the summer, when we were out of school, I would ride along with Dad out into the coal fields. On one of these trips we were near Logan, West Virginia, on a gravel road. We stopped in a coal company store for lunch. There were no McDonalds or fast food places in the early '50's. The store sold just about anything you could imagine and had merchandise literally hanging from the ceiling. In the corner was a small lunch counter with about four chairs. Behind the counter was the door to the toilet. The door was made of several pieces of wood, with one running diagonally to prevent sagging. From behind the door we could hear the cook taking a leak that sounded like he hadn't gone in a long time. He came out, wiping his hands on an apron with stains of all colors that had accumulated over several weeks. He asked, "What can I get you boys?" We said we wanted two hamburgers, and he asked how we wanted them. Dad said, "Just fry the piss out of them."

The first building Dad's business was in had previously been a barbershop built into a hillside. The building was quite small, but the price was right - $35 per month. The primary sales items were cash registers, which were quite large and heavy. Space was at a premium.

Dad hired his first technician at this time, a fellow named Percy who had learned to service office machines at a place called Moundsville, or the state prison. Percy was attempting to organize the back area to conduct a service operation when he encountered a problem. The hot and cold water coming into the area had been capped off, leaving the copper caps sticking about ¾ of an inch out of the floor. When moving around in the area, Percy would trip on the caps. A local gave him a price of $20 to bust up the concrete floor, cap off the pipe, and refill the concrete. Percy explained this to Dad in great detail and asked if Dad would take care of it. I can still picture Dad as he stood there, bow-legged, straw hat and short cigar in his mouth, frowning. He said, "Percy you can stump your ass on those pipes and I won't pay $20 to remove them."

The second technician he hired was a rather large fellow that weighed over 300 pounds. The weight factor isn't significant unless the fact that he drank too much is taken into consideration. To prevent his being off work because he was hung over, he was given an extra $5 per week for not missing work. This money would accumulate to around $20 or $25 a month, and was referred to as the drunk check, because when he received this check he was off a few days. The drunk tank in Charleston was on the second floor. There was no elevator, so this technician had to be carried by the police officers up the steps on a stretcher. On one occasion they dropped him. I guess 300 pounds was a little heavy. He probably avoided arrest a few times as the police officers dreaded carrying him up the steps.

There were consumer loan companies around Charleston, each with a loan limit of $800. The state increased the limit from $800 to $1,500 in the mid '50's. This second technician had a bad credit rating but paid one loan company on time and was given a certificate from them saying he was golden. He took the certificate to all the loan companies and received max loans of $1,500 at each. Upon receiving this, he disappeared for a month. His poor wife was grief stricken but held onto hope for his return. A little over a month later he called, apologized, and said he was going to jump off of the South Side Bridge and end it all. The wife called the police and went to the bridge, hoping to stop the suicide. He wasn't there and had not been seen by passersby. When the wife returned home, he was in bed. He still knew how to return home to a sympathetic wife. A few years later he passed away and Dad went to the funeral.

There were seven or eight people at the funeral home to see him off. Three of the people attending were women, leaving four men, so Dad became a pallbearer. That became a problem because of the weight of the deceased. As the pallbearers strained to carry the casket to the hearse they had a stairway to descend. Dad said the dead man slid in the casket, putting most of the load on the lower two carriers. They almost dropped him. The hearse was an old Packard with a floor shift. The only person who could drive a straight shift was Dad, so he became the hearse driver. At least the preacher showed, so Dad didn't have to do that, too.

Dad, my brother Joe, and I went fishing in Poca, West Virginia, a small town about 25 miles down the Kanawha River. We were fishing on the Pocatalico River. As we fished off in the distance we kept hearing a muffled "Whump!" That is my best description for the sound. Nothing was said about the strange sound until it began to get louder. "What in the world is that sound?" Dad exclaimed. Just as he said that a boat with three fellows in it emerged from behind an island. They would light something and throw it into the water, then the "Whump!" sound. They were fishing with dynamite, which is kind of like fishing with shrimp, minnows, and worms, etc. The difference is you can't miss. We watched as they rowed by, as they had no outboard motor. It was not a fancy bass boat like you see today. As they passed by, they rowed over to us and asked if we wanted some fish. "Absolutely!" was our answer, and they gave us about ten carp, suckers and catfish. The bass, blue gill and anything worthwhile they kept.

After fishing for about three hours we decided to go home because nothing was biting. Guess the fish were all shell shocked. We put the fish on a stringer as if we caught them ourselves, we loaded the car, and headed for home. Not far down the road we stopped for Dad to get some cigarettes and beer, "very important." The place where we stopped was a shack about fifteen feet off the road. The building was about twelve feet deep and if you stepped out the back door you would fall about fifty feet to the railroad tracks below. Dad carried the fish into the place on a stringer and told them the fish were really biting that day. One guy asked Dad what we were catching them with and Dad said we caught them on a hula popper.

Funny thing is that of the fish we had on the stringer, none would be caught on a hula popper because they weren't game fish. We had a hula popper in our kit, and it was worthless, never caught a thing on it. Half the men in the beer joint got up and headed out to fish.

Dad had a number of West Virginia business axioms. I wish I could remember them all. Here are a few:

Trying to motivate a lazy employee is like throwing a tin can behind an old hound dog. He will speed up for about 3 or 4 steps and slow back down again.

Never invest in another man's business. If you are not your own best investment you're in the wrong business. Nobody will pay you as much as you will pay yourself.

If you want to have money in business, don't spend it.

The easiest way to go broke is by trying to please everybody. There are some that will never be happy regardless of what you spend.

Always act a little dumber than you really are. It makes it harder for somebody to get over on you.

Selling to country stores required sales ability, the right personality, and above all, tactics. Dad invented most of his tactics and, of course, they fit the environment of the day. I walked into a store with Dad over near Logan and he had an adding machine to sell.

He wanted to get $150 for it. Dad walked around while the store owner waited on a customer. The owner looked at the adding machine and asked how much Dad wanted for it. If Dad had said $150, the owner would have said, "That's a little steep, how about $110?" and they would haggle to an unsatisfactory finish. Instead, Dad looked at a moldy ham hanging from the ceiling and said, "I love a good ham. Tell you what I'll do. The price for the machine is $180, but I'll give you $30 for that ham." The owner was more interested in swindling Dad with the rotten ham. He forgot about the $150. He handed Dad the $150 and the ham, and we left. Dad was whistling and singing (I hated his singing) and drove away. We stopped about 200 yards up the hollow and Dad threw the rotten ham into the creek.

CHE-CHE

My father opened a cash register business and operated it from our home until finding a suitable location. Several technicians and sales people were regular visitors. One sales representative, Opie, brought his young daughter when visiting. His daughter was Che-Che. He had a Spanish look with the thin mustache and dark hair. But like the rest of us he had a fine West Virginia twang in his speech. His daughter was quite young, about two years of age. My brother, sister, Che-Che and I decided to play hide and go seek. I was around four years old and we were all quite young. Che-Che and I hid under my mother's dresser. The dresser was about three feet wide and two feet deep. It had no drawers and only a top for the application of makeup. The sides and front were draped with fabric, allowing the two of us to fit underneath. We obviously had to be small for both of us to fit.

Having a little problem with gas that day, a little slipped out. As the smell worked its way into the area, it was embarrassing. To cover my tracks I said, "I think I smell potato chips." The small child, who had just recently started speaking, looked up and said, "It smells like a fart to me."

HIGH SCHOOL INCOME

In high school I loved to have a few dollars in my pocked to pay for movies, food, clothing, etc. Since there were no handouts from my parents, it became apparent I would have to make the money on my own. My dad owned a cash register company in Charleston and would have technicians come in from local companies. He had service technicians from NCR, Monroe, Burroughs, etc., come in on Saturday mornings to rebuild used cash registers and repair customer machines. The number of machines they completed each Saturday was usually one. I would go in on Saturday morning and dismantle, chemically clean, and paint registers for $5 each. Five dollars in the 50's was a lot of money. As an example, Dad paid a local guy five bucks one Saturday and he got a haircut for $1, eight gallons of gas for $2, a bottle of wine for $1, and a car wash for his last $1. He was ready for Saturday night in Sissonsville.

My objective was to complete two machines each Saturday and make ten dollars. In addition, I wanted my Dad to recognize me as a man, which he did not do until years later. It was, "Tommy, go down to the corner and get me a coke." This lack of recognition finally caused me to go to work for his competitor across town while still living at home. Dad was a fantastic salesman, always number one when working for insurance and cash register companies. His drinking brought all these jobs to an end, so he went into business for himself. When dealing with a disgruntled customer, he had ways of getting back at them without raising his voice or being argumentative. As he listened and dealt with the complaint he would repeatedly mispronounce the disgruntled customer's name, while maintaining a calm composure and straight face. By the time we left, the customers were so pissed off they were talking to themselves. The ones he hated most were large, overweight women. After dealing with a customer of that description, as he would leave the store, I would hear the words, "That old porpoise!"

There were problems while riding around with Dad. The first was his singing. Driving through the deep valleys and hollows in West Virginia, there was little or no radio reception, so he would sing. His favorite song was, "I Found a Million Dollar Baby in a Five and Ten Cent Store." He never even came close to the actual notes and was guilty of severe ear pollution. The second problem was his chain smoking with the windows up on cold, snowy days.

His doctor told him to start smoking cigars, thinking he wouldn't inhale them. He, of course, continued to inhale, and the smoke became even worse. Burning ashes from cigars are much larger than those from cigarettes, so now he had burn holes in all his white shirts and ties.

After Dad passed away, Mom made me a vest of his ties, with the burn holes included. I wore it every Christmas day as my children opened their gifts. It became a family tradition.

At one point Dad became interested in vitamins and asked an old country doctor what he thought they would do for him. The doctor replied, "Can you fertilize a field with a fart?" Evidently, he had no faith in the tiny pills and Dad forgot about vitamins.

Across the street from Dad's store on Bigley Ave was a restaurant called Humphrey's Dairy Bar. The owner was a very strict German with no sense of humor. Dad, his business partner, and a couple of retired salesmen that hung out there each day, would plot and set up jokes on the fellow that would take weeks to set in place. Over a period of time, bits of information would be dropped by Dad and his cohorts, who would discuss each step at the shop. Finally, they would drop the bomb, at which time Humphrey would have a drastic reaction. The shame is that I can't remember the plots.

There was an alcoholic that walked up and down

Bigley Ave with a wooden box full of paint cans and brushes that hung from his shoulder by a piece of rope. This was long before computer generated graphics and lettering. His depth of alcoholism caused him to shake very badly. To make money he would paint store names and advertising on store fronts. Dad said that he was the only man he had ever seen who could shake a straight line.

After I got married and left West Virginia, Dad would call me every Sunday evening. I, too, was now in the office equipment business in the Washington, DC, metro area. We would tell each other about the deals we had made the previous week. As salesmen often do, our stories were often embellished just a little. The embellishment could, in some cases, render the story to be a little less than true. I sent Dad a small round IBM typewriter element. The element never was delivered to Dad and he said, "I know what happened to that element, the Post Office employees stole it. They thought it was an apple!" Whenever I received no call I knew Dad was not feeling well. After Dad passed away, I continued the Sunday evening calls with Mom. There was one phone in her house, and as she grew older the number of rings increased before she answered the phone. I then installed a phone by her chair in the living room and another by her bed. Mom lived to one hundred and three years of age. She drove a car, bought groceries, and paid bills well into her 90's.

When calling I would ask what she had for dinner that evening. Her reply always started with, "Why do you always ask me that?" Many of her older neighbors would cook a pot of beans and eat only that for a few days until they were consumed. Mom's dinners consisted of some meat, green vegetables, starch, and even a small dessert. Many of the vegetables were from her own garden. This contributed to her health and long life, I am sure. One evening when she answered the phone I asked her, "What number were you dialing?" She answered, "It must have been zero if I got you." It was hard to grow up in Dunbar with a sense of pride.

Mom had two major interests in her life, tapestry hooking and raising beautiful flowers. Her yard was so beautiful that artists would come to her garden in the spring and summer, set up their easels and paint. Her children and grandchildren all have beautiful paintings of her yard, and tapestry hooking gracing our homes. A composite of paintings of her yard and home were sold to Senator Jay Rockefeller and hung in his office on Capitol Hill for years. A picture of mom with two of my children visiting the office is attached.

If you asked Mom the name of a flower in her garden she could give you the Latin and the common name, the number of them in her garden, and the location of each. She was quoted on a regular basis in the local newspaper on gardening and fishing. This was something for a widow in her 80's and 90's.

It was her desire to promote tapestry hooking and gardening. When urging others to try tapestry hooking she was often told that it was just too tedious, but they pronounced it "tee-juss". Mom hated that word, so I managed to work it into our conversations as often as possible. She always received it with sharp return comments.

She was a member of the Arborvitae Garden Club in Dunbar. Arborvitae is a shrub and means friendship. When discussing any garden, I would work in comments about arborvitae, which once again drew an angry stare and comment.

In trimming Mom's yard once, I cut her lilac bush down to the level of the rest of the bushes. This really irritated her, and she commented on it for days. In her later years, Mom was living in Houston with my sister. She had several mini strokes and was no longer conversational, but I think mentally she was still there. My sister said that Mom could no longer remember much about her home and was pretty much out of it. I told Mom that I was going back to Dunbar and going to check on the lilac bush. She very sharply commented, "Whatever is left of it." I also told her after visiting Dunbar that there were very few flowers in her yard but the neighbor's yard across the street was beautiful. Her comment was, "He doesn't have the gumption."

Mom liked to have a drink each evening, which my sister would not allow because of the prescriptions Mom was taking. She wanted just one, never more. She was sitting very quietly one afternoon and asked me out of the blue, "Tom, could you get me a beer?" I said I would and went to the store for a six pack.

As a widow through her 80's and 90's living in a small house in Dunbar, West Virginia, you would expect her to be invisible, but her comments were often in the local newspaper and even in an airline magazine. A friend of mine was flying from Florida back to a class reunion and read about Mon's garden and the paintings in an article published by the airline. He gave me a call and sent me a copy.

HOME BREW

This next story could go into the category of "Live a lot and learn a little." My neighborhood friend moved in at the age of four. His name was Gary, and he was one year younger than me. Since we were close in age we began to play together. As I recall, we liked to sit around and plot about what kind of pranks we could pull against our neighbors. At our age we were only allowed to travel a couple of blocks from home, which limited our list of victims. Our efforts to play innocent were unsuccessful, so soon our parents forbid us to play together.

In high school we were both drummers in the band, marching side by side, and out of our parents' control. My older brother and a few of his friends had taken a five-gallon sulfuric acid jug from the abandoned glass plant in Dunbar. They cleaned out the jug and used it to make home brew. Gary and I decided to take some with us on the bus to a football game to be played in Barboursville, West Virginia. We secured a gallon glass jug and filled it with the home brew. The two of us quickly drank the gallon early on in the ride. The alcohol content must have been minimal because we felt no effect. However, the urge to pee was screaming. Riding at around 35 mph on West Virginia roads with sizable pot holes and a suspension system that gave you a jolting feel with each pothole was excruciating. Near the end of the trip, Gary's face was red, and he had tears flowing from his eyes. I'm sure I looked the same. We were about to go to the back of the bus and find a bass horn case to relieve ourselves but fortunately we arrived at our destination. Two streaks from the bus to the toilet happened as soon as the bus stopped.

My memory of this event, even though it was close to sixty years ago, still brings pain.

DUNBAR BAND

As a proud member of the Dunbar High School Marching Band, we really enjoyed many ball games, concerts, trips, and competing with other local bands. The band had over a hundred members plus majorettes. Our drum rank used the largest diameter drums, which were equipped with concert snares to make them louder. We used triple S sticks, which were the largest available. The sticks made our drum beat somewhere close to thunder. We were the Dunbar Bulldogs. On occasion, we would form the stick figure of a Bulldog on the field at halftime. Our lineup had a clarinet player placed where the two hind legs met the backbone. To make our bulldog anatomically correct, the clarinet player would hold her clarinet slightly forward on a downward angle. I don't believe the band director ever saw this.

In concert season, the band was crowded into an annex to practice. With the small space and over a hundred instruments, the volume was so loud you could feel your clothing vibrate. The instrument storage room was behind the drum rank. Occasionally one of us would slip back there while the band was practicing. A large variety of spare instruments were stacked around, including an old bugle, bells, saxophones, etc. We would pick one up and blast off with a squawk, blat, or whatever. Our director, in spite of the extremely high volume, would always hear it and stop the music. He would then spend about five minutes berating the trumpet section, trombones, or whoever, asking them what they thought they were doing because they sounded like a grade school band. The members of that section would look at each other with looks of disbelief, not having any idea what had happened.

I thought our director was a little on the effeminate side until discovering he was a belly gunner on a B-17 during World War II. That changed my opinion.

GRANNY FISHER

In the east end of Dunbar lived an eccentric old man we all called Granny Fisher. He drove around town in an old REO truck. His driving speed was somewhere above a brisk walk. When he drove by, if going our direction, he would allow us to hop on the back. He would then caution us with the words, "Hang on boys, I'm gonna run 'er up to fifteen!"

He had been written up in the local papers for some of the things he had done. One article told of his deciding his REO was too powerful and burned too much fuel, so he removed a piston and replaced it with a piece of wood.

He ran a saw mill on his property. An article about his starting the motor on diesel fuel and switching over to natural gas after running went into some detail. He had built a stern wheel river boat and would gather logs from the river during high water or flooding. By the time I saw it, the stern wheeler had sunk in front of his house and saw mill, with only the wheel house sticking out of the water. I was there one day when he fired up the mill. After starting the motor, he moved a large lever and the whole building began to shake. A large steel shaft, with belts leading off in many directions and running from one end of the building to the other, started spinning. The building was made of slab lumber from the mill. No two pieces were the same. After the motor started and the drive belts engaged, the building must have swayed at least a foot from side to side. If OSHA had been in existence then and witnessed this, they would have run out screaming as if seeing a ghost.

While walking around his house with him one afternoon there was a beautiful Mallard duck lying beside the house that been mauled by his German Shepard. He looked down at the duck and said, "I wondered where he was."

My mother sent me his obituary a few years after I moved away from Dunbar. He had started as a concert pianist in New York City before moving to Dunbar, West Virginia. What a guy!

GUN POWDER

A group of my friends in Dunbar came across the ingredients to make gun powder. The new gun powder of today is pretty much smokeless and burns at a high rate of speed. The combination of ingredients my friends received produced the old black powder used years ago, which smoked heavily, and burned a lot slower. They loaded a piece of pipe with some of their powder and drilled a hole in the side of the pipe for a fuse. They nailed the pipe to an old shed and concocted a makeshift fuse. After several unsuccessful attempts to get the fuse lit, they devised a new method. They heated a two-foot piece of wire cherry red on one end and placed around a corner of the shed into the drilled fuse hole. The blast took off part of the fuse handler's sleeve, as well as the shutters off of a neighbor's house. Fortunately, they were not at home.

After this, the group gave up the on explosions and looked for another way to use the gun powder. One participant said he had an idea of how to use the remainder of the powder. They filled a plastic cup with the powder and took it with them to the local town theater. They emptied the cup's contents into an ashtray inside the movie entrance where patrons who smoked would snuff out their cigarettes. They walked a few steps away and stood there to watch. A few minutes later, after entering the theater, a patron placed his cigarette in the ash tray. The tray immediately blazed with a flash, scaring the poor patron. He yelled and jumped back. The smoke from the powder filled the theater and forced its closing for about an hour to clear the smoke.

LIGHTING SEWERS

The town of Dunbar had its streets and sewers laid out during the depression era by the WPA. Streets were paved, water system built, and a cavernous sewer system laid under each street, dumping into the Kanawha River. We read in a local paper that someone had set off a firecracker next to a sewer entrance on a street corner, causing the methane gas from the sewer to ignite with quite an eruption. We thought we needed to try that, so we lit a piece of paper and dropped it next to a sewer entrance at the corner of West Virginia Avenue and 20th Street. The ground shook, one-inch steel plates rattled and danced, it was great. When a car passed over the plate in the middle of the road a blue flame would be pulled about twenty feet out behind the car. We lit the sewer about once a week until my buddy Gary had a bad experience. He had four brothers and lived in one of the few houses on the street with a basement. Five boys meant a lot of dirty laundry lying on the basement floor. Gary's Dad was a devout Christian and attended church every time the door opened. He had never uttered a curse word in the presence of the family. When Gary arrived home after one such sewer lighting there was a noisy commotion in the basement. His Dad was standing in about four inches of sewage that backed up due to our igniting the sewer gas. The sewage was soaking into the laundry lying on the floor. His Dad was uttering an endless litany of curse words, possibly for the first time in his life.

We waited until he was over the age of eighty to admit our crime.

JUNIOR HUNTING

Two guys from Dunbar, West Virginia, loved to hunt. Whenever they could, they would go into the hills that surrounded the town. They hunted small game, which included squirrels, rabbits, quail, etc. Their names were Tom and Biggie. Most of the guys in town had nicknames, and Biggie was probably given his as he was the biggest guy in Dunbar. They would meet up at Ross's Pool Room and head out to the hills from there.

A pool room regular named Junior wanted to go hunting with them. There were two problems with Junior. The first was that he did not have a shotgun, and the second was that he had never been hunting. I never knew Junior's last name or where he worked as he was in the pool room every day. Another pool room regular loaned him a shotgun, so he informed the boys he was ready.

Tom and Biggie said they would take him but were concerned about his lack of experience. He knew nothing about common safety rules and might shoot somebody. On the way up the hill into the woods there was an open field with a large apple tree in the middle. They told Junior since it was his first hunting trip they were giving him the best spot. Of course, he was told this to keep him out of the woods and keep them out of danger. They put him in the open field and told him everybody knows squirrels love apples. They then proceeded on up the hill and hunted for a few hours, killing or seeing nothing. On the way back down they picked up Junior, who had four squirrels.

ROSS'S PIZZA

In a small town, when a stranger walks into a business they may as well have a big sign on their back saying "Stranger." On a few occasions a stranger would walk into Ross's and order a pizza. The pool room did not serve pizza or much of any other food. You could get potato chips and a few similar items, but that was about it. Bud Ross would produce an order pad and take the pizza order. Details were written on an order pad he kept there for this purpose. The customer would be asked about everything that could be asked if really taking an order. Thin crust? Extra cheese? Pepperoni? Onions? Mushrooms? Pineapple? Sausage? Small, medium or large? And on and on. Once the order was completed, the ticket was placed under the counter and the Ross's would go about their business. In ten or fifteen minutes the customer would ask about his order. Bud Ross would get a concerned look, bang on the mirror behind the counter, and once again go about his business. After three or four times banging on the mirror and yelling, "Where is that pizza?" the customer was told, "Sorry, we're out of pizza."

ROOKIE COP

A local boy, nicknamed Smokey, had been a regular at Ross's for years and was known by everybody. A good guy, liked by all and accepted as one of our own, he became a cop in the neighboring city of Charleston. After going through all the training and being placed on the force, he came in wearing his full uniform. The uniform was new, the badge shiny, and his weapon in the holster. From the first minute he stopped in everybody started teasing him. Where did you get the costume? Are you going to a Halloween Party? Look at the plastic badge! How heavy is that cap gun? You even shaved and brushed your teeth!

After about fifteen minutes, Smokey became fed up with the verbal abuse and asked them politely to shut up. When the guys kept on with the abuse he reached down, pulled his gun, and shot a few beer bottles off of a shelf. If that happened today the FBI would become involved and it would be front page news. Back then the guys thought it was great and asked for a second shot (which did not happen).

The teasing stopped.

RED TAILED HAWK

In our town the favorite place to go was Ross's Pool Room. As a teenager, we could go in, play pool, see all of our friends, but no beer until we were of age. There was no fooling anyone on age, as in this small town you knew everybody, where they lived, their brothers, sisters, cousins, and how old they were. When going out on a date we first went to Ross's, then on the date, and stopped by Ross's on the way home. On the walls on either side of the pool room were shelves spaced about ten feet apart. The shelves had been used for fans before the building was air conditioned. Once air conditioning was installed, the shelves were used to hold empty beer and soda bottles placed there by people playing pool.

One day there was a large red-tailed hawk sitting on a shelf about halfway back. When I asked who killed the hawk, the answer was nobody. The large hawk had swooped down on a small hunting dog and the dog's owner threw his hunting jacket over it and brought it to Ross's. When entering the pool room, he released the hawk, which flew to one of the shelves and perched there. The hawk stayed on the shelf for a day or two, ate some hot dogs, and started flying around scaring the patrons. Finally, they opened the front door and the hawk was ushered out.

FARTING CONTEST

Whenever a large group of men ranging in age from 16 to 60 gather on a regular basis, it is natural to have competition in many areas. In a pool room, of course, playing pool is the main competition. But not all have the needed skills to be competitive. The male mind is constantly looking for ways to compete and especially in areas where they excel. Therefore, considering the above and the fact that many men and boys are superior at this skill, a farting contest was initiated with the following names and scores (to the best of my memory): 12 – Phantom, 10 – Trombonium, 8 – Trumpeter, 7 – Cheek Flapper, 6 – Tear Ass,10-Hand Off.

The Phantom received the greatest number of points, a 12, as it required the greatest skill. The first requirement was to silently emit an adequate quantity of gas to create odor. This was to be done with a facial expression of pure innocence. In addition, you must position yourself close to others for maximum effect.

The Trombonium, scoring 10 points, was audible and included a change of tone (usually starting high and going lower). Facial expression was not required.

However, you needed to position yourself close to others to be sure of receiving proper recognition and points.

A Trumpeter would score 8 points. This must be performed in higher pitch with intermittent tones.

A Cheek Flapper would score 7 points. This required even fewer skills. It just needed to be loud with audible flapping.

A Tear Ass, scoring 6 points, required the fewest skills. It was usually loud but required the proper diet.

A Hand Off, scoring 10 points, was not a fart, but the ability to fart and successfully blame the person next to you.

Contestants were listed on a wall board and scores recorded on a daily basis.

GLASS PLANT PIGEON

A large hand-blown glass manufacturer, named Dunbar Glass, closed down in Dunbar in the mid 1950's. After closing, literally nothing was removed. There were five-gallon jugs of sulfuric acid at various places throughout the plant. We emptied a few and made home brew in the jugs. There were also fifty-five-gallon steel drums filled with arsenic in a few areas. We were with a doctor's son who we considered to be a mad scientist. He told us if we mixed arsenic and sulfuric acid it would burst into flames. We then threw a handful of arsenic on the ground and poured sulfuric acid on. Poof, we had flames.

A couple of years later an extra edition of the local paper came, stating the arsenic had disappeared and if thrown in the river would kill everything down river. Don't know if they ever found it.

There was a tower that rose about 50 feet above the factory. The tower had windows around a square enclosure, and the only entry was a trap door into the bottom. The tower was inhabited by a number of pigeons. We could climb the ladder and enter through the trap door without allowing the pigeons to escape. One Saturday on our weekly trip to the Price Theater, we climbed up and grabbed a pigeon and put it under a coat. The pigeon did not show through the coat, and we entered the theater without a problem. We released the pigeon inside the theater. It flew around, hit the screen, and crapped on an unlucky moviegoer. The camera was a carbon arch light and extremely bright, making the pigeon look like a shooting star.

There was a very large warehouse on the river side of the plant. As we strolled through, we would see large owls, mice, and a few other inhabitants. Union Carbide had nearly filled the warehouse with spools of a fabric called vinyon. The warehouse was beside the New Salisbury Bridge, which became the Dunbar Bridge when May or Salisbury left office.

A local doctor's wife jumped off of the bridge, committing suicide. Under the bridge were several boats dragging the river in a recovery attempt. Mac, our mad scientist, knew what a drowned person looked like in the water, and directed our construction of a vinyon-filled dummy using some clothes left in the warehouse by a homeless person. We carried the dummy upstream and placed it in the water where a stream entered the river. On the riverbank a fire department member was tending a fire that the searchers would occasionally use to warm up. We walked over to the fire as innocent observers. A few minutes later, when the dummy came into view, the fire tender saw it and started calling to the search boats. They were all excited until they realized it was a dummy.

The dummy made the front page of the local paper. I wish I had kept a copy.

DEAR ABBEY

One of our favorite activities in high school was to write letters to Dear Abbey in an effort to get them published. Usually three or four of us would gather in study hall and pool our ideas. The first thing we would do is come up with a scenario. The scenario would be as preposterous as we could invent, with a tinge of believability.

Of course, we wanted the letters published, but we also wanted Abbey to be asking herself, "Dear God, what is happening to our society?!" or "Do people this stupid really exist?"

We completed about one every two weeks as our writing was interrupted by studying for tests and other useless pursuits. My memory is pretty good, so I will try to recall a couple of examples.

Dear Abbey, I have been dating Mary for about a year now, and at first, we were really in love but as the year has passed this love has cooled. We really need to part and go our separate ways, but there is something holding me there. She has a beautiful cat that I love dearly, and the cat feels the same about me. Mary couldn't care less about the fantastic animal and gives it no attention at all. If I am totally honest about our situation do you think she would give me the cat? Or do you think I should steal the cat and tell her it ran away? Also, the poor Kitty is pregnant and it's for sure Mary would not take care of the kittens. – Signed, Bewildered

Dear Abbey, I recently met the most beautiful woman whose black hair, dark eyes and olive skin caught my attention and I can't get her off of my mind. She seems to like me. We went to a movie and out to eat last week. Where ever we went she turned heads. There is a problem, however, that I don't know how to approach. Her Middle Eastern heritage includes eating many spices and ingredients that produce body odor. The bathing habits of people in that area are somewhat less than ours, which of course multiplies the difficulty. While in a restaurant the other night the group at the next table got up and moved to the other side, away from us. She invited me over for dinner with her family the other night, and even though my allergies dampen my ability to smell, the stench was overwhelming. In addition, the food caused me to have excess gas. She and her family have no problem expelling gas whenever needed. How do I approach this problem with her and her family? Would buying perfume help? – Signed, Befuddled

NAP

In the stories I've written this has been held until the very last. The reason is that the things that went on in the 1950's regarding Nap would be frowned upon today if not considered criminal.

Nap had a less than normal IQ and was the source of a number of creative situations. As I look back I do not remember him being treated with negative names, taunting, or things of that nature. It was just the opposite, as everyone liked him. Dunbar was a small town, and everyone knew him on a first name basis. He could walk into the mayor's office and be greeted by name. He worked at the local pool room racking pool balls, sweeping, taking out the trash, and a few other such duties. Looking back, I think the job was created for him to give him some money and something to do.

A local country singer and radio personality sponsored a talent contest to be held at Dunbar High School. Nap was convinced that he could sing, so he was entered in the contest. The pool room bought him a guitar and an embroidered country shirt to wear when performing. He was taught one cord, and before performing that night his fingers were placed on the strings. As he walked up on stage to perform, he tripped on some large power cords and lost his cord. He just gripped the guitar with four fingers across the strings. The song was monotone, "Sittin' At Home All Alone, on My Telephone, Don't be Cruel" just like Elvis. The audience went wild – screaming, yelling, and whistling. You couldn't hear a thing until he was finished. The winner was decided by applause. When a hand was held over Nap's head for applause the response was deafening. This was a shame as several of the contestants could really sing and had no idea of what was happening. The guys from the pool room filled half the bleachers and poured down around the audience and up onto the stage. They lifted Nap up onto their shoulders and carried him off the stage and out the door. The show was held by Sleepy Jeffers, who was saying loudly over the microphone, "The show isn't over! The show isn't over!" He also was clueless as to why the gymnasium was full. As everyone was leaving he was trying to sell autographed pictures of himself. Nap had become the King of Rock 'n' Roll, and teenage girls would scream and run over to get his autograph when they saw him in the street. The guys in the pool room would help Nap write songs and would gather around him in a writing session. I am sure you can imagine just how well written the songs were with no tongue in cheek inferences. After the songs were written they were posted on the pool room wall for all to read.

A few years later I had a two-week assignment in Manhattan, New York, servicing typewriters. While in a music publishing company I noticed new songs hanging around on the wall. I couldn't believe it, they were no better than the songs composed in the pool room.

JERRY

There was a fellow in my class at school named Jerry. His life was pretty much the same as the rest of us in the little town of about 10,000, called Dunbar. We attended Dunbar High School, took various jobs for spending money, hung out at the pool room frequented by younger guys, went hunting on the local hills when we could, etc. Jerry was from a large family, which included several cousins and uncles that were older guys. A couple of his uncles worked on cars and always had a few extras on hand. Jerry, who had no car, would borrow one from them as needed. He frequently borrowed an old 1948 Kaiser that was about ready for the junk yard. The car had been recently repaired but all the parts had not been reinstalled. The most obvious part omitted was the hood. While driving through Roxalana Hollow en route to Dunbar, Jerry didn't make it around a sharp turn and ran off the road into Bess's Supermarket. He was soon surrounded by police, fire department, and many curious locals. We never knew if speed, condition of the '48 Kaiser, or alcohol were contributing factors. In the investigation the question regarding the location of the hood became a focal point. Jerry said he saw it flying up and over the store. The firemen produced ladders and climbed on top of the building in search of the hood. They also checked the creek and surrounding yards. The final conclusion was that someone had stolen it.

DOOR SHOCK

Our friend, who we called the Mad Scientist, picked up a Model T Ford coil. The coil, when connected to a dry cell battery after starting the vibrator, would throw a bright spark about an inch and a half. The voltage was very high and would shock you severely. The amperage was low, so even though you received a substantial shock there would be no damage.

In discussing how we could put the coil to use, we decided to run wires to the passenger side door of our '49 Plymouth. Then we started driving around picking up hitchhikers. Well, not picking them up, but giving them quite a shock when the door was grabbed.

We learned a week later that one such hitchhiker wasn't mad about the shock, but because we did not pick him up. When attending a high school reunion recently one of my classmates mentioned our shocking him. I had forgotten and was happy he remembered.

BOB YMCA

A neighbor of mine named Bob and I decided to get our Life Savers Certificates and apply for a job at the local 4H pool. We had to travel to the YMCA in Charleston, West Virginia, for the course, which took several nights. As we were driving through Capital Street, which was the main drag in Charleston, Bob was throwing out popcorn down into the street to attract the pigeons, where cars could run over a few. This, of course, would cause the female shoppers to become somewhat nauseous. No, I can't explain it. This is what teenage boys do.

When being tested to determine our swimming skills, we had to hold our arms out of the water and stay above water using only our feet for a couple of minutes. One of the guys being tested was a poor swimmer and was going under and gasping for breath. We started laughing and nearly drowned with him.

The instructor called for a volunteer to step forward so he could demonstrate artificial respiration. This was performed at that time by laying the person face down, sitting on their legs, and pushing on the rib cage in slow rhythm. Bob quickly volunteered to be the victim. Bob was instructed to lie face down, which he did. The instructor then sat on his legs and applied pressure to his rib cage. Bob immediately cut the loudest fart I have ever heard. It echoed off the tile walls. The demonstration quickly ended.

MOM BROOM

In our family of three children, the one receiving over ninety percent of corporal punishment was me. Our next door neighbor had a large hedge between our two properties. I can't remember them ever trimming the hedge, because so many switches were cut by my Mom.

One day Mom was sweeping the front steps with a broom. She asked me to come over to her, as I had once again broken some rule of conduct. After thinking about it, I turned and ran the other way. Mom threw the broom. Rounding the corner of the house I was hit in the back of the head by the broom handle. I wasn't disturbed by being hit in the head by the broom but was impressed by her skill. Until her dying day she was told if the Olympics held a Broom Throw event she would be a winner. She was also informed that child abuse charges were being filed. She denied it all.

GUN BARRELS

On Tyler Mountain, near Dunbar, there was a custom barrel smith that made gun barrels for rifles, pistols, and shot guns. The barrel stock used was all the same length and after being drilled and rifled would be cut to the proper length. This would leave pieces as short as a few inches or over a foot. We would pick up pieces of a foot or more, thread one end of the barrel, put a bolt in, and drill a primer hole in the side. We would load the barrels with black powder, lighting it through the hole in the side to fire the gun. We used a drill the size of the barrel bore to make holes in a 2x4 piece of lumber. We melted lead into the holes to make bullets. We would load a twelve-inch barrel about half full of black powder, wadding, and a lead slug. We took the barrel to the Kanawha River bank to fire out over the river. When firing, we all hid behind trees and the unsecured barrel would fly about twenty feet backward. We aimed at an old Jon boat across the 150 yard river, but never came close.

MACK – BOAT

One of our friends in Dunbar was the son of a local doctor and a brilliant young man. At Christmas he was given a fourteen-foot boat with a ten-horsepower outboard. This may not seem like much today, but to us in the '50's it was the Queen Mary. We spent many days on the Kanawha River, hunting, fishing, and exploring the local streams that flowed into the river. In addition to the boat, Mack had a collection of muzzle loading guns. Mack and I had gone downstream to a back-water area below Dunbar to shoot floating bottles and other things of interest. We were returning to Mack's home upstream at a speed of about ten miles per hour as we passed the home of a fellow we knew. In a small town you know everybody. It was Bob Pignatto, who ran down to the river's edge and while laughing began throwing sticks, rocks, boards, and anything lying around. We were about twenty feet off the river's edge and easy targets. Mack had a forty-five-caliber muzzle loading pistol that was double barreled. He had loaded firing caps and powder but no shot. He pointed the gun at Bob and fired. Bob's eyes flashed in fear and he began running away. He was more afraid than he normally would be as everybody thought Mack was a little crazy. As Bob topped the upper banks, Mack fired again. At that point I'm sure he needed toilet paper. I saw Bob a few days later on the Main Street of town and we both laughed about it. Today there would be helicopters, Coast Guard, and FBI summoned to the scene. Back then we laughed.

16th Annual Commode Bowl Classic
Thanksgiving Day, Nov. 26, 1970
HILLSIDE vs. RIVER RATS
(All-Time Champs)
(Small Time Chumps)
DONATION
OUR PRICE
.50c (cheap)
Lions Field
2:00 P. M.
Rain Date-Nov. 26, 1970
Drawing held at Half-time For FREE Chance to have Nap Vicker spend Christmas with you. Plenty of Room At
Sec. A Row S Seat S

COMMODE BOWL

Each year in Dunbar there was a traditional sandlot football game. At first it was called the mud bowl and was held at various places around town, most usually on a very muddy lot. As time passed it became known as the Commode Bowl, and was played every Thanksgiving Day. The age of the players ranged from early teens to the thirties, for anybody who wanted to play. A railroad track runs through the middle of town, and became the dividing point for team selection. The Kanawha River borders one side of town, and hills border the other side. Players from the river side were called River Rats, and those from the hill side were called Hill Siders. At one point the uniform for River Rats included a yellow streak down the middle of their backs. A few games were held on the practice field at the high school, and one year everybody climbed the fence to play on the football field.

As the game gained popularity it had a full acceptance and was allowed on the high school football field. There was a pregame parade that included cars and garbage trucks from the city, and was on the radio. Both teams had bands and a Miss Commode Bowl was crowned at half time. As industries died down in the area and the population dwindled the game suffered for lack of a sponsor. When urban renewal removed half of the downtown area and Ross's Pool Room closed, the center of communication was gone. Ross's Pool Room had sponsored the event, and since all the guys spent time there, they would plan the game and enjoy talking about past games while razzing the losers.

When action on field was dull, there was hootenanny in stands.
STATE MAGAZINE, DECEMBER 8, 1963

River Rats, Hillside Rams to play in Commode Bowl

The River Rats will take on the Hillside Rams in the 32nd annual Dunbar Commode Bowl Thanksgiving day at Lions Field in Dunbar.

A parade leaves Murphy Mart at 11:30 a.m. following a circuitous route along West Virginia Ave., 23rd St., Charles Ave., 22nd St., Fairlawn Ave., 12th St. and Dunbar Ave. to the high school.

Admission to the game is 25 cents. All proceeds will help provide a Christmas to disadvantaged children in Dunbar.

I THINK IT'S FUNNY ...

HARLEY RIDE

While in high school, a buddy acquired a 1946 Harley Davidson motorcycle. The motorcycle probably weighed over eight hundred pounds with all the accessories, crash bars, and thick steel used in 1946. The bike had a kick start and a handle control to retard the spark before starting. If you tried to kick start the bike and did not retard the spark it could backfire and throw your leg up into the handle bar, causing serious injury. The bike was so heavy it was all I could do to bring it up right from the kickstand.

A classmate of ours, who had always wanted a motorcycle, was sitting on it with the motor running. His mother, who was older and very sickly, didn't want him to have a motorcycle. She was older, probably forty.

The bike had a suicide clutch which was spring loaded, and when tilted forward would spring down and engage the clutch. As the classmate revved the engine, one of the guys kicked the clutch down and the bike lurched down the street. About fifty yards away the road went down over a hill and we lost sight of him. We stood there laughing and waited for him to reappear. After waiting about ten minutes with him failing to return we started walking in that direction. He was coming back pushing the bike. When asked why he was pushing instead of riding, he showed us a house at the end of the street. Apparently as he was turning he goosed the bike and hit a two-foot rise at the yard edge. He flew through the air and hit the house about halfway up the wall. The house was covered by asphalt shingles and we could see a few broken where he hit. A line of tangled shrubbery stretched across the front of the house. He and the bike fell into that. Fortunately, nobody was home so he dragged the bike from the shrubbery and was pushing it back to us. I have no idea what the occupants of the house thought when returning home. I bet every picture hanging inside had fallen. That ended his desire for a motorcycle.

JACK

In my public speaking class in high school, there was a classmate named Jack M. He was a large fellow for high school, weighing around 250 pounds. In contrast, my weight was, at that time, around 130 pounds. I did continue to grow for a few more years, reaching six feet and 225 pounds.

Jack and I were given an assignment of conducting a debate with the question, "Is Rock & Roll detrimental to the morals of teenagers?" We decided that, regardless of the winner, we would fake a fight (which is why the weight difference was mentioned). We both were given one of the girls in the class as teammates. My side was to argue the music was bad, and the winner was to be decided by the applause of our classmates. My team predictably lost.

Our teacher was around five feet tall and was frequently seen in front of the school with an extremely long cigarette in her mouth, an interesting contrast. At the end of each day we would audibly count down to the bell and run for the door as a group. Our diminutive teacher would stand at the door and push back whoever got there first, and they would fall back over chairs, onto the blackboard, or whatever.

She had the impression that she had complete control and never sent anybody to the principal.

After the debate the students gave Jack's team the victory. Jack looked at me and said, "Well, Tom, we beat you fair and square." My comment was, "Come on, you can't expect these people to agree with our side." Jack answered, "Are you saying we weren't good enough to win?" He then grabbed me and we began wrestling around in front of the class. Our teacher grabbed Jack's shirt, pulling him backwards. As he moved back, he fell across her desk and all we could see were two large legs sticking up behind the desk kicking. She told us to take our seats once again, thinking herself in complete control.

At the end of the year we took up a collection to buy our teacher a present for doing such a good job. Jack went to each member of the class and amassed one dollar and fifty cents. The money was taken to Miller's Drug Store on Twelfth Street, where he purchased a five-dollar box of chocolates. Being short three dollars and fifty cents, Jack had to charge the balance. The 1950's predated credit cards. Instead, you simply gave them a name and address for the balance. Jack gave them our teacher's name and address. When we gave her the candy she was so touched she cried. When receiving the bill, she probably cried again.

The school mascot was a bulldog, and we had a coach that looked more like a bulldog than any human should.

I understand he previously played for an NFL team. He would be described as a large husky man with no neck. When teaching the class, he would frequently speak with incomplete sentences. We were given a test which included essay questions. I answered the questions using mostly incomplete sentences, and was given an A, plus positive comments written in the margin.

One day he announced he would be gone for a week and we would have a substitute teacher in the interim. The substitute was to be given instructions to report any misconduct in the teacher's absence. My friend Jack must not have heard the warning and committed some infractions of the rules. Upon returning, the coach called Jack to the front of the class and reminded him of his previous instruction. Our class was in a wooden annex building which was pretty flimsy. Coach grabbed Jack by his lapels and bounced him off the blackboard. It sounded like a bomb went off and shook the whole building. The teacher from the adjacent room came running in wide-eyed, asking what happened as Jack staggered to his seat. We hear that this type of treatment is extremely detrimental to the development of young people. When Jack was married, a few of Jack's friends pulled three of his six spark plug wires before he limped off to his honeymoon. He raised two daughters, had a successful marriage, built and owned a welding business while being the pastor of a local church. Jack was a great guy!

MY BROTHER'S MED SCHOOL

My brother, Joe, attended medical school at the University of Kentucky in Lexington. The members of his class were a diverse bunch and included a group of three very intelligent young fellows. Their intelligence combined with confidence led them into a few embarrassing situations. One of the guys had a girlfriend who owned a large parrot. The parrot's toenails had grown long and needed to be clipped. This need led the group of three to volunteer to perform the operation, after all they were doctors. The bird was large and was quite aggressive when approached by someone other than his owner. The group fabricated a small cone-shaped piece of plastic to be a mask, enabling them to administer ether. When the bird was unconscious its nails were clipped. One of the nails began bleeding and they could not stop the bleeding. They then decided to cauterize the wound to stop the bleeding. A parrot's bones are hollow to make them light. Ether is highly flammable and explosive. When cauterizing the wound the bird blew up.

One member of the group had a dog that had

gotten very sick. Their medical lab had a large quantity of medicine and this group decided to bring the dog in for a treatment. After administering the medicine, they had concocted, all of the dog's hair fell out. The dog was then housed in a container with nuclear symbols to ward off prying eyes. The dog's hair did grow back, and it survived. The group, due to their intelligence, felt superior and would make remarks about their fellow students' stupidity. This usually drew the comment, "How is the bird doing?" This story may seem farfetched, but it was given to me as true!

ARMY MEDICAL

The first part of the process of joining the army was signing a large pile of papers. The papers must have covered every subject known to mankind and would have taken the first year of our enlistment to read. I have no idea what I agreed to do or not do. Our depth perception was tested on a long tray about two feet wide by ten feet long. Two pieces of wood were on ropes and you were tested by pulling until the objects at the far end were side by side. A friend of mine had poor eyesight, so I stood by the table with my hands by my side and signaled by moving fingers to indicate the direction he should pull the ropes. Blood pressure, heart, the paddle in our mouths and all other areas were checked. Next was the questionnaire covering other aspects. When asked whether I was right or left handed, the answer was I don't know. I write with my left hand, throw a ball with my right hand, shoot guns right handed, and play pool left handed. The doctor looked a little disgusted. He had about 50 more guys to check, and snapped, "Which hand do you masturbate with?" I held both my hands in front of me and said, "Both." He grunted and wrote something. No idea what it was.

ROYAL TYPEWRITER

While working for Royal Typewriter Company in Charleston, West Virginia, the cast of characters working there made it most enjoyable. First of all, our janitor, who was quite large and not the cleanest guy in town, smoked a pipe. When we discovered the pipe sitting around on a bench we would cut up rubber bands and place them in the tobacco. The rubber bands looked just like the tobacco, so when he picked up the pipe and lit it black smoke would begin to drift upward, accompanied by an "Awshit!"

We sat on wooden work bench stools that were cupped out with butt-shaped depressions for our comfort. One of the cleaning agents we used to clean typewriters was alcohol. Alcohol, when poured onto the top of these stools, was almost invisible. Our janitor, or anyone else sitting in the alcohol, would stand up and do a dance that would make Michael Jackson jealous.

One of our technicians continually carried a coffee cup, sipping throughout the day. When finding a full cup sitting around, we would drop in a greasy platen ratchet, which was a greasy piece of steel just over an inch in diameter. When the coffee level got low enough, the ratchet would roll down and hit him on the nose.

This same fellow bought a Volkswagen Bug and would brag about the mileage. We would pick up the Bug and place in on the sidewalk and various places. One day we put a starter bomb on the engine. These wonderful devices would whistle loudly, put out a ton of smoke, and end with a loud bang. What we didn't know was that his wife was coming to pick up the car that day. Adding to his misery was the fact that she had a terrible temper and was very domineering. We were all watching to see him leave on a service call when the wife walked in and took his keys. At this point we all retreated back to our benches while he stood in the window smiling. She turned the key, causing the loud whistle, smoke and bang. We all ran out to see what happened and saw the car filled with smoke. All we could see of her was the outline of silver glasses. Her interpretation of the event was that her husband did this, as he was standing in the window laughing. He was in the dog house for about three weeks.

The door to the restroom had a gap at the bottom a little over an inch, and if you stayed in there too long the person waiting outside would take action to shorten your stay. The drum containing alcohol was next to the door with a can on top used to take the cleaner out. This can was filled, poured under the door and set on fire, causing a quick reaction inside the toilet. There was a large mop in there that I would place across the opening inside the room. On a few occasions smoke drifted up from the mop while in there.

We had a salesman named Roy who thought he was Elvis. He had the hair, the loud clothes, and would walk around singing, making us all nauseous. He was always broke and borrowed ten dollars from a technician. Whenever we were all together the technician would ask, “Where is my ten bucks?” just to embarrass the salesman. On payday the technician would stay out on calls when Roy had money, and of course he was broke the next day. This lasted for about six months until Roy finally came up with some money.

Next door to Royal was a greasy spoon restaurant and we ate lunch there about every day, plus went back for coffee and snacks. In the back of the restaurant was a narrow doorway that led into a room filled with chalkboards, as it was the gambling center for the city of Charleston. We knew the bag men who traveled around the city picking up the cash and information on a first name basis. The owner was a guy named Big Ed, who had a wad of cash in his pocket as large as a softball. On payday we cashed our checks next door, and Big Ed peeled off a few bills. Ed’s wife ran the restaurant portion up front. She was a large woman with quite a temper. Big Ed realized this when they got into a fight and she shot him. The wound was superficial, and both were back to work shortly after the event. Taking advantage that at this point Ed had become gun shy, we would set off a few cherry bombs just outside the screen door leading to the alley. One person would light the cherry bomb while the others would be inside to watch Big Ed jump.

In order to purchase a coke, we reached into a cooler below the counter. As we picked up a coke there was a carton of raw eggs close, so we would also get one and carefully drop it into the bowl of hard-boiled eggs on the counter. I was never there to watch an unsuspecting customer try to peel a raw egg. One day the place was raided, and as Big Ed and friends were being led out in handcuffs our service manager, Tom Dodd, was standing in the front door of Royal watching the arrest. It appeared on the newscast that he was being arrested, too. Tom grew up in Charleston, went to school there, and knew a lot of people. That evening, Tom's wife received a number of calls from friends whose conversations invariably led to, "Well, how is Tom?" These calls really irritated Tom.

ROYAL CHRISTMAS

In 1968 I became the District Service Manager for Royal Typewriter in Washington, D.C. Our office was located at Wisconsin Avenue and R Street. The area was just above Georgetown, crowded, with little or no parking. Our brick building had five departments: Commercial Service, Commercial Sales, Government Service, Government Sales, and Supply Sales. There were five Christmas trees in the basement, one for each department. I wasn't aware that a trip to the basement was necessary to secure a tree so I was the last one to go down and get ours. The remaining tree was the worst looking excuse for a tree you could imagine. It had about half the limbs, the tree trunk was bent, and most of the greenery was gone. Looking at this sad excuse for a tree I could have requested a new one, but the light bulb came on in my brain. I decided to decorate the tree with typewriter parts and red and black typewriter ribbons. The decorations enhanced its forlorn appearance.

We also had rules for gift giving. The cost of the gift must exceed twenty-five cents. The gift should be a gift of meaning, i.e., if the person you are buying for is fat then the gift should point that out. If the person you are buying for has occasional body odor then some perfume would be appropriate. We drew names, but you were not restricted from buying additional gifts of meaning for others. The objective was to receive as few gifts as possible. As I recall, the first gift I purchased was a Fleet enema. For our party, the presents were placed under the tree and a punch bowl with various juices and booze of several types was prepared. One fellow that camped a lot was given a funnel attached to a gallon jug to eliminate his trips out in the dark to urinate. Our party was so loud with laughing that the other four departments all came down to watch. We had the best party in the building.

LEAF COLLECTION

In a biology class, we were given an assignment to prepare a notebook featuring samples of leaves from fifty different trees. The samples were to be pressed, glued and properly identified. A notebook of fifty leaves or more would be given an A, and lower quantities would be given lower grades. The class was walked around the town of Dunbar through various yards where many types of trees were growing. We were given strict orders against returning to the yards to retrieve samples, as the owners would complain, and the next class would not be able to return the next year.

Upon getting out of class the day of our tree tour, a buddy of mine named Bobby (who later in life became Bob) asked me to drive the two of us around the route while the trees were fresh in our minds. I was one of the few kids with a car, as I had lied about my age and gotten my driver's license at the age of fifteen. As we were getting in the car, a rather obnoxious and pushy classmate said he wanted to go with us. We will call him Breezy, which was not his nickname, but its close enough. We proceeded around the route traveled earlier, getting samples of each forbidden tree. While driving down an alley, Bobby said to stop there. This was puzzling, as there was only an open field there with no trees. Bobby ran out into the field and pulled three stick weed leaves. When he returned, he said they were called Blue Pippen. He handed each of us a leaf and started writing the name in his notebook. I knew it was a stick weed leaf and trashed mine. A little further down, he again told me to stop. He ran into a field, grabbed three sumac leaves, came back, and told us they were Yellow Doves Beak. We, of course, faked writing them down and proceeded on. Another fake leaf was added to the list, for a total of three. The assignment was handed in a week later. Breezy had his total of fifty leaves, so he was expecting an A. The next day, our teacher, Bugs Tosh (the Bugs part was given to him by the students) called Breezy to the front of the class. He was complimented on his creativity. However, he was given a B, as the three fake names were not accepted.

ARMY M41

When in the Army, we used to go to the USO functions, which were held about once a week. The USO would bring in young nurse trainees from a local insane asylum. Training at an asylum was part of a much larger course and lasted three months. Several guys from my outfit would watch the girls as they came in, and grade them in the following categories. If the girl was thin she became an M41, which is a light tank. If a littler larger and pretty normal in height she became an M48, or medium tank. When heavy, the girl was classified as an M60, or heavy tank. A girl came in one night that was over 6 feet tall and quite buxom, obviously an M60. That night we were with a short guy who was around five foot six. He was a Russian immigrant whose nose was a little shorter than he was tall. His name was Shellpac. As a joke we asked him to go dance with the M60. He thought it was a good idea and went over and began dancing with her. His nose was between her boobs as they danced. Wow, that was funny. After dancing, he returned and we all laughed and kidded him. A little later we asked,

"Hey, where is Shellpac?" He was back over there dancing with the M60.

He married her! We all hoped for his sake that he never pissed her off. She was big.

MAGS AUTO

After high school, several guys formed the Mags Auto Club. Mag is short for magneto, and I have no explanation for why the club was named that. We had Model A Fords with Cadillac, Chrysler, Oldsmobile, Studebaker and Chevrolet engines. We also built dragsters to take down to the local drag strip. We had blue jackets with our club name on back and actually lived what you see in some modern movies. We rented a large garage in the East end of Dunbar, and about anything you could imagine in tools were there.

Most of the members of our Mags Auto Club were guys we had known most of our lives. We had known Donnie since elementary school (the last name has been omitted due to legalities). He could be described as always smiling, overactive, laughing, and everybody liked him. After purchasing a '50 Ford coupe he joined the local fire department as a volunteer. The purpose of joining was to get the red lights and siren. In riding around with Donnie, if someone pulled out in front of us (or we saw a carload of girls), he would turn on the red lights and siren and pull them over. Then he proceeded to walk up to the driver's window and start yelling, cursing, and waving his arms for added emphasis. This continued for about six months, until he pulled over a constable in an adjacent town. Unfortunately, he then lost the lights and siren.

In a period of two years, Donnie tore the transmission out of the car over twenty times. After having the repair done a number of times and watching people repair the transmission he became very proficient at the repair. He had three or four used transmissions laying around for parts. One evening he came into the Mags garage and hooked the back bumper of a car to a chain hoist and lifted the rear of the car so high he could walk under it. When told he needed to put something under the car in case the chain broke, he pulled a Model A Ford under the car, that's how high it was. We told him if the chain broke it would be like a mouse trap. He disassembled the transmission, put in parts from his stock, and was out of there within two hours.

JIM DATES

After high school one of the guys got a job in Charleston at a popular shoe store. As various girls from the towns in the Kanawha Valley would shop for shoes he would make dates. Sometimes the dates were with just one girl and he would go. Other times there might be as many as four, so he would ask the guys and we would all go.

One date, in St. Albans, West Virginia, was with four girls. Jim, my brother, another guy whose name I don't recall, and I went on the date. About three minutes after our arrival, Jim got into a fight with his date, so that was over. My date was a beautiful blonde with which I was thrilled. She was not only beautiful, but her parents owned a large shopping center and she came from money. However, I learned she was fourteen years old, so that was over. The third guy's date was a dud, which left my brother. My brother married his date.

Jim and I were to go on a date with two girls from Stonewall High in Charleston. Evidently, he found something better and told me to find a replacement for him at the last minute. Everybody gathered at Ross's Pool Room before going out, so I went there looking for somebody with nothing do to. There was only one guy there with nothing to do, and his name was Windy. He was excited and asked me to take him by his house so he could shower and change clothes.

I waited out in front of Windy's house for about a full three minutes. Windy came out wearing the same clothes. The only difference, he now smelled like Aqua Velva and body odor. When we met our dates, mine could have been a weight lifter on the Russian Olympic Team, and she was the prettier of the two. I could see why Jim had backed out. The date was short-lived.

JOE MILAM

Between semesters in college I worked for a civil engineer in Dunbar named Joe Milam. We were given various assignments around the state. Our first was to survey a rock quarry out Sissonville Road. We were surveying down in a valley and the rock was being quarried on a hillside above us. We were instructed that when the horn on a pickup truck was blown three times to look up. The horn blew three times followed by a gigantic blast. When looking up, we saw a sky full of rocks descending down on us. Our defense was to step aside to avoid being struck. As teenagers, we had good eyesight, coordination, and full faith that we were invincible, so we stepped aside when needed with absolutely no fear. We were not even protected by today's thin plastic hard hats.

Another assignment was to survey the town of Ravenswood. The previous survey had been done many years before by an inaccurate system using chains. As we began, nothing was where it should be. When placing monuments for street corners, they were always a few feet off. As we proceeded down each street, fences and hedge lines from one homeowner were on a neighbor's property. Many of these people who did not like the fence, hedge, or the neighbor, would proceed to cut or tear them down. This caused serious problems along every street. One day the fellow operating the transit said, "Oh, God, look at this!" Looking through the transit there was a house dead center in a street.

When running levels for coal seams on mountain sides, we would encounter small mines dug by people from the area. Some were dug to sell the coal and others to heat local houses. In front of the mine shafts were wooden boxes for supplies and dynamite. A fellow worker took a couple of sticks of dynamite, blasting caps, and a fuse. He placed two sticks of dynamite in the barrel of a World War I canon on a local college campus. A one-minute fuse was lit and the perpetrators drove away. Upon hearing a loud blast, they drove back. People were out there milling around but there was no police presence. Everyone knew it was a prank back then and went on with their lives. This was in the late fifties and none of the perpetrators are with us today.

BEAMAN MANUFACTURING

The Fletcher Enamel Company had been in Dunbar since the turn of the century. The machines there were massive and had no safety devices whatsoever. They produced enamel pots and pans that lost market share for a period of time, so they closed. Now they are imported from Mexico. In the late '50's, Beaman Manufacturing Company leased the place and equipment to produce gas station facades for nearly all oil companies. We produced sheet metal facades covered with porcelain of all colors. Esso red, Gulf blue, Shell orange, Texaco green, and of course, white and complimentary colors. The foreman there was a hunting and fishing buddy of my Dad's and gave me a job.

My friends and I were just out of high school and building hot rods. Under our hoods were air cleaners, battery boxes, and many parts covered in colorful porcelain. I was one of the few employees there that had all my fingers. The massive presses that were used to form metal had no straps to pull hands clear when coming down. One machine came down to within one quarter of an inch before hitting bottom. An employee had his thumb under the press, and after being pressed to one quarter of an inch it looked like a beaver's tail. It did recover over time and looked normal.

Unlike today, the attitude was that if you stuck your finger in a machine and were injured you weren't a victim, you were stupid.

The sheet metal came into the plant with a light coating of oil to prevent rust. After cutting, forming and welding, the metal had to be cleaned before the enamel could be applied. There was a small building with a concrete floor and two large, square holes in the floor. These were filled with sulfuric acid to dip and clean the panels before applying enamel. There were no railings, warning signs, or restraints in the room. To walk in there and step in a pool of sulfuric acid would have been a serious deal.

When holding a small piece of metal in one hand and an acetylene torch in the other, I burned the end of my index finger. An acetylene torch will melt steel, so the burn was third degree. The torch was so hot it immediately killed the nerves and did not hurt. The finger was ugly and smelled very bad, but when you are a teenager you think anything will heal.

A shop foreman who applied first aid to me said, "O'Daniel, you are being very brave about this." It didn't hurt and I didn't think it was a big deal. I looked up and said, "I can take it."

EAST END FRIENDS

In the tenth grade of high school I bought my first car. It was a 1936 Ford two door sedan. The price was $50 and I drove it home from Anstead, West Virginia, near Hawks Nest. If you are not from West Virginia I'm sure the names mean nothing. There is still a cloud of smoke trailing down the Kanawha River from when I drove it home. The car had been driven many miles as there were no new cars built during World War II. I worked on it for a solid year, rebuilding the engine and drive train. 1936 Fords were supposedly capable of going eighty-five miles an hour. After adding dual exhaust, dual carburetors, new rings and a few additional items it would do more than eighty-five in second gear, but it took a while to get there. The paint was done with a brush and was kind of a frog pond green. I did nothing to the exterior. My friends, the Payne brothers, had a 1940 Desoto four door sedan. Another friend, Larry, had a 1950 Plymouth. We could drag race these cars in front of the local cop. We only had one cop in the town, and we were so slow he would not realize we were racing.

One of our favorite things to do was to get on the practice field by the high school after a rain when the grass was slick. After starting side by side, we would all three whip the steering wheel to the left and spin side by side across the grass. It was a beautiful thing.

Once when driving toward Dunbar, Larry and the Payne brothers were driving behind me. The guys were in the front seat and some local girls were in the back. I would see the car swerve a little from side to side and hear screaming followed by a "Whomp!" Larry was throwing firecrackers into the back seat with the girls. After graduating from high school, Larry ran computers at Cape Canaveral, Florida, and became the mayor of West Melbourne, Florida.

VIRGINIA BEACH

While living in Virginia Beach, Virginia, for three years and working with a group of young guys, we became very good friends. We would attend softball league games that several of them played in, go crabbing on Lynn Haven Inlet, and fishing in the Chesapeake Bay. In addition, we dug clams in Rudy Inlet and drank beer in a few local establishments. Growing up in West Virginia, this was all new to me. After gathering a number of crabs and filling a bushel basket, we would boil them in a pot laced with spices. It didn't matter how many we caught, they were all consumed. The clams we gathered in the fall were cherry stone, small and delicious.

Most of us were employed by Royal Typewriter. Royal had a publication to which all branches contributed. The publication solicited sales tips from all branches. We, of course, contributed. We took a picture of a salesman with a group of IBM typewriters spread out on the lawn in front of him. His back was to the camera with his legs spread about a foot apart. He appeared to be urinating. The caption was, "Royal Salesman gets relief from IBM." Another sales representative was attempting to sell machines to a bank headquartered in Norfolk, Virginia, with no success. We were drinking beer one evening and the purchasing agent walked in and made some smart remarks to our sales representative. The sales representative popped him in the mouth, which ended the conversation. The next day, the bank ordered three machines. Both occasions were submitted to Royal as sales tips, but for some reason our suggestions were never printed.

Once a month we would gather with the wives and cook dinner. One month the wives would cook and then next month the men cooked. One evening the men had a roast in the oven and a complete dinner on the way. When we bought the roast we also picked up a beef tongue. While the roast was cooking we were rolling the tongue around on a butcher block dusting it with flour and pounding it with a meat tenderizer. We told the wives that would be our dinner and it was a penis.

They would walk by the kitchen door and look in with a fearful frown.

KICK IN REAR

A rather large young fellow who worked for me at Royal Typewriter Co., in Norfolk, Virginia, was encouraged to go out for football in high school. After a year of constant urging from the football coach he relented. As part of the coach's persuading, he had promised weight training as well as all needed mental and physical instruction. After joining the team, this fellow did receive great training from the staff overseen by the coach. The coach was very passionate and, therefore, demanding and angry at all times.

Due to this fellow's size, he became a defensive tackle. On the practice field after a play he felt something hit him in the rear. He turned to see the coach limping off of the field. Coach had kicked him in the ass so hard that he sprained his ankle and limped around for a week.

CHARLEY

A good friend named Charley worked for Washington Gas in Northern Virginia. His job consisted of making calls on residences and businesses. The calls would include installing meters, connecting and disconnecting service, etc. To accomplish this, the van they used was full of heavy equipment.

Charley was a large man with a normal temperament and did well with his family and friends.

The van had a crew of two men, Charley being the lead because of his technical knowledge and experience. He was accompanied by a driver who aided Charley on the calls.

The driver was ex-military and had served in the Middle East. While serving there he was recruited into a religion that believed you would come back after death as the living being you killed the most. Every time a squirrel, bird, or cat would run in front of the van he would jam on the brakes, throwing heavy equipment to the front of the van. The equipment would, of course, end up hitting Charley.

Totally disgusted with this, Charley grabbed the driver by the nape of the neck and dragged him to the front grill of the van. He said, “Look at the front of the van and the hundreds of dead mosquitoes plastered there! That is what you will be; now get back in the truck!”

RED CROSS BLOOD MOBILE

My office equipment business in Fairfax, Virginia, made its money primarily on service and sale of rebuilt machines. In Washington, D.C., at the Navy Yard, there was a weekly sale of surplus machines that we could purchase for around $30, and retail after being rebuilt and repainted for between $399 and $499. Having no financial backbone when starting the business made this amount of markup allow me the option of trading for needed equipment of various types. One of our trading partners was the American Red Cross. They were the recipient of various donations from the C&P Telephone Company, Virginia Electric Power, and several others. They were an excellent source for cars and trucks for use by our technicians and delivery people.

On one occasion, they had acquired a new blood mobile and were interested in trading the old one for some used IBM equipment. After some haggling over what would be traded, the deal was made. Upon picking up the Blood Mobile, I was asked to remove the signs that boldly displayed the Red Cross symbol and Blood Mobile signs. Of course, I agreed. I drove home to check it out, and determine a price to resell the truck, as it was not really useful to my business. While driving home, I began to feel that, "Hey, this is funny!" feeling, and decided I would leave the signs on for a few days.

Upon arriving home, my three children were loaded on board for a trip through our town to get some ice cream. The bus was driven all over the place for about a week. We even drove it to church and parked right in front.

While talking to the Director of the Red Cross (a very shy and soft-spoken gentleman) on my next visit, he said that one of his people had seen the bus being driven with all of the signs still on. My answer was, "Nooo! Really?" Fortunately, the bus was sold the day before, and the signs removed.

SARAH

I hired a young lady as a receptionist to answer phones, deal with customers in the showroom, and receive service calls. She was also to type letters and handle anything else that needed to be done. She had come to the U.S. from Pakistan and spoke perfect English, as her parents had worked with the Embassy of Pakistan. She had a terrific telephone voice and dealt very well with the customers that walked in. Her sales of machines and supplies over the counter were far above any other person in that position. Her short coming was in typing, as she would leave out sentences or transpose words. It was decision time, as she could no longer remain in the receptionist position. I decided to try her in sales and assigned some existing accounts for her to work as she made the transition. She took this very seriously and worked them and a few more vary hard. Before her sales began coming in she would come to the shop in the afternoon highly irritated that the customers weren't buying. She was around five feet tall and would walk in stomping and frowning in disappointment. Her sales took off after a month or so, and she received a nice commission check. She came in a few days later and told me of using the check to buy some new clothes and was excited at saving over $200 because of a sale. I said, "That is great! Do you realize what you have done for your husband? He now owes you the $200 you saved, which you can take out and save him another four hundred!" She got a serious look on her face, as if thinking, Yeah!"

Within a couple of months her sales exceeded the numbers posted by two older, more experienced salesmen. They became very jealous, which was apparent by the way they looked at her and made comments. The worst thing they came up with was that she was unprofessional.

One month after experiencing low sales numbers, I announced that we would be having a sales training session on Saturday morning, and that Sarah would be teaching. The other two salesmen didn't smile.

Due to her height, she could barely be seen in her car when driving. There was a big tank farm a few blocks away from our store, so large gasoline tank trucks were constantly driving by. Everybody made fun of her driving. With her visibility and driving skills, the very fact that she is still alive, there has to be a God.

One snowy day she was in early and I received a call from my service manager saying it was so slick that he couldn't make it in. He lived about two miles away and drove a four-wheel drive pickup. I told him it wasn't a problem, because Sarah was in the office and would be able to come and pick him up in her Chevrolet Vega wagon. He slammed the phone down and was in the office within five minutes.

DELIVERY TRUCK

When opening my office equipment company, the money was tight for the first year. After six months in business our service of customer machines became quite busy, and it was apparent we needed a delivery truck. A new business of one year has no credit and very little money. The local post office was selling delivery vehicles for $900. We scraped together the money and bought an old van from the post office. The van was old, slow, burned a tank of gas every day, and had no air conditioning. Our driver hated it.

I had the bright idea of bolting a typewriter to the top for some free advertising. My idea would have the typewriter in the center above the windshield. One of the sales people said instead we should bolt it on a back corner, so people would think it was inadvertently left there and forgotten. We did bolt it to a back corner, and also painted it red so it would stand out from the blue truck.

Once the typewriter was bolted to the top of the truck, the driver left for deliveries and we forgot about it. Three days later I asked the soft-spoken driver if anyone had noticed it. His eyes rolled back, and he started with, "You cannot believe the attention." He had caused wrecks as passing cars would be honking the horn and pointing up and hit another car. The police had pulled him over to complain but could do nothing about it. One delivery was to a four-story building. People on all four levels above were pecking on their windows and pointing.

We removed the machine to avoid legal action.

COPY ROOM FART

While working in my office, the problem of excess gas raised its head occasionally. Since I'm there alone, the gas is released, and I continue working thinking nobody will be the wiser. However, a minute or two the odor hits me and also the realization the statement that mine don't stink may not be true. Shortly thereafter the door opens and one of my female staff walks in and hands me something to sign or has a question. There is no recognition of the odor and the exit back into the hall is rapid.

After repeating this situation a few times, the need to take steps to avoid it became apparent. When repairing a copier in a customer's copy room the need to avoid embarrassment was on my mind. The room was large, and I was alone, so I released what I thought to be a small amount of gas. It may have been a small amount, but it was lethal. In proceeding with the repair, I heard the sound of footsteps off in the distance. My escape was to walk across the hall into a kitchen area. Two ladies came around the corner and walked into the copy room while I observed from across the hall. I walked into the room behind them and said, "Woah!" The two became red faced and left.

DEER

One December in Northern Virginia was extremely cold, which isn't out of the norm, but we had below freezing temperatures for about three straight weeks. In the town of Manassas Park someone hit a deer in a residential area, knocking into someone's front yard. The owner of the home being a fellow West Virginian and accustomed to using the material at hand realized the frozen deer could be used in his Christmas decorations. The deer was stood up and decorated with lights. Of course, he placed a large red light on the deer's nose.

The stance of the deer was not exactly normal, as it was hit from the rear, causing the back to be bowed up and the head to be in a lower than expected position. When viewing this grotesque decoration some of the neighbors began to complain to the gentleman who set it up. They cited the odd appearance and concern for their children. Very appropriately, my fellow West Virginian told them to get lost. Complaints were then directed to the local authorities, who said there was nothing they could do. After a couple of weeks, he was cited for not having a game stamp and the deer was removed.

In January he was summoned to court for proper adjudication. The prosecutor, a young lady, who was viewing the pictures of the dead decorated deer to present her case, started laughing. Unable to stop laughing, she handed the pictures to the judge. The judge also began laughing and told the perpetrator to get out of the courtroom.

GARAGE DOOR OPENER

An attorney friend living Manassas, Virginia, regularly worked out with a group at a local gym. The group consisted of friends and a former classmate. The conversations generally consisted of anything that would bring a laugh and was rarely of any serious nature.

One evening my friend had a garage door remote control in his pocket as he was to deliver it to a relative in a couple of days. Upon discovering the remote control in his pocket, he pulled it out and pretended to think it was a pager and that he was receiving calls.

The next day he was in court before a judge who worked out with us, a school mate and good friend. Unfortunately, his client, who was a fellow West Virginian, didn't show up. The judge was from Alabama and loved to berate my friend about West Virginia. He made several negative remarks about the state and the client. An onlooker in the courtroom who did not know any better would think they were bitter enemies. A bench warrant was issued for the client along with a few more negative remarks. My friend turned and began walking out. About halfway out, he stopped, turned around toward the judge, and pulled out the garage door remote control. He then said, “Sorry your honor, I thought it was my client calling.” The judge put his face down on the bench and struggled to mask his laughter.

SILVER REED

For several years I was a dealer for the products of a Japanese company in Los Angeles. The name of the company was Silver Reed, a division of Silver Seiko. The employees were a mixture of Japanese and Americans, with a friend of mine in charge. Whenever you called the company, the nationality of the person answering was quite obvious. The receptionist would answer with a very clear, "Sheeva Leed," my phonetic spelling of how she pronounced the company name. The Japanese people are quite proud of their race, and consider themselves to be a little brighter than most others, which I can't argue. One morning as this receptionist answered with her "Sheeva Leed," I commented, "You have the cutest accent! Are you Mexican?" Her answer was an angry, "No! Nipponese!" When she connected me with my friend he was told of my comment. I thought he would swallow the phone he was laughing so hard. It seems he sensed their opinion of him in frequent conversations.

RICHARD

A good friend of mine and neighbor in Sterling, Virginia, had a father who was suffering from arthritis. The father was very talented in making grandfather clocks, tables, and many other items, which were given to family members. While making these items his hands were stretched, moving in a very therapeutic manner. In addition, the wood used for these projects was chestnut. The chestnut was from before the great blight that killed all the trees in America. A quite large stash of the wood was kept in a barn where the family originated in Tennessee. Needing a method of hauling the wood to Northern Virginia, my friend bought an old white Cadillac hearse.

His wife did not like having the hearse parked in front of the house, but every now and then he would park it there. One evening a few guys were laughing about the hearse and hatched an idea. A member of the group worked for the Army Mapping Service and made two signs out of white plastic with an adhesive on the back. The signs read, “Miller’s Mortuary – You Plug Em, We Plant Em.” The car and the sign backgrounds were white, so when attached to the two front doors it appeared the letters were painted on. Fortunately, the hearse was parked in front of the house on the night of application of the signs. When looking out and seeing this in the morning, a desperate phone call was made to Mr. Miller. He was in California that morning, and thought it was funny. When he came back home he did not remove the signs.

A couple of weeks later I was given a story by Mr. Miller that I could not believe. As the Millers were driving through Danville, Virginia, on a four-lane highway, they noticed all cars in the other lane had their lights on. The other lane was a funeral procession. As they proceeded, the lanes merged, putting them into the procession. They continued in the procession until they came to a couple of policemen directing the procession into a cemetery. Mr. Miller almost ran over the cop, whose mouth was open, not understanding why the hearse would go straight. I thought the story was contrived until given an account by his wife, who told the story with clenched teeth, It seems she had gotten down on the floor to keep from being seen in the procession.

A couple of years later I helped by selling the hearse to another resident of our area. When delivering it, the wife and young son of the man who made the purchase expressed their displeasure at having a hearse in their driveway. I began extolling the benefits of this fine vehicle to gain their approval. When explaining that the radio would only play hymns I lost them.

PSYCHIATRIST

My office equipment business in Fairfax, Virginia, had a showroom with a display window in front. The receptionist was also in front, to greet customers and answer the telephone. Behind a partition across the room were work benches where the technicians repaired the various types of office machines. Shelves to hold customer machines and our stock were behind the technicians. My office was up a short flight of stairs at the back of the store. On occasion I would see my receptionist and a couple of my technicians hiding behind the shelving peering at the front of the store. When seeing this, I knew a local female psychiatrist was in the reception area with her typewriter to be repaired.

This woman, who probably weighed about a hundred pounds, always had an angry scowl matched with obscenities for effect. None of my employees would wait on her. They would all retreat to the rear of the store.

I would go up front and say, "Oh, Dr. X, how wonderful to see you! (Name omitted to prevent legal action). You look wonderful today!" She would give me a look of complete disbelief. "What can I do for you?"

She had an IBM Selectric typewriter that would print dashes if the keys were struck too forcefully with bad timing. This was a problem that could not be fixed, and IBM offered $100,000 to anyone that could. In viewing the problem, it was always the same, printing dashes on a letter to her sister. Every time we ever checked the problem, it was on a letter to her sister. Maybe her sister had mental problems!

My employees knew what would happen next. I would call for the technician who had most recently screwed up an account or done something stupid to come to the front of the store. She would meet them with her signature scowl and obscenities. Her anger was compounded by the fact that the problem could not be fixed. After attempting to fix the problem, I would carry her typewriter to her car and thank her for coming in. To my memory she was never charged. The last we saw of her was before it came out in the local news she had been arrested for practicing without a license.

OUT OF IT PARENTS

After my first marriage ended, my three children came to live with me. While attending my twenty-fifth high school reunion, I was reunited with a lovely former classmate who was also in the process of a divorce. I had known her from the first grade and she became a wonderful addition to my life. She also had three children, which gave us the Brady Bunch. We were both around 43 years of age. We were young, happy, and full of energy, but as far as our teenage children were concerned we were totally out of it. Anything we did regarding humor, music, dancing, etc., would cause our up-to-date children to want to hurl. Realizing there was no way to change their opinion, we decided to go with it. When using the expression "Right on", we would say, "Right arm." For the expression "Far out" we would say "Farm out." A popular song at the time was Electric Avenue. We would sing "Electric Have a You." Any song that was played on a regular basis became fair game for our word changes. Nothing, however, could approach the embarrassment generated when we would dance.

When combining the exclamations, modified song words, and our dancing, they would leave the house. The very best time for these displays was when they had friends over. The level of embarrassment reached supernatural heights during these periods.

GENE

A friend of mine living in Manassas, Virginia, owns a large garage that repairs about anything with wheels. In addition, he watches Craigslist for profitable vehicles he can purchase, repair, and resell for a profit. He buys cars, trucks, motorcycles, boats, and tractors. An ad appeared for a car with an estimated $10,000 retail price and a purchase price of $2,000. When calling the seller, he found the vehicle was located near Richmond, Virginia, which is about two hours south of Manassas. The potential profit caused him to decide to make the trip. On the way south, he began thinking about some reports of dishonest people luring cash-carrying buyers in with a profitable offer and robbing them. Nearing Richmond, the directions led him off the interstate onto a two-lane country road, causing him to think even more about scammers.

The drive made him a little thirsty, so he pulled into a gas station restaurant. It was the opening day of hunting season and the lot was filled with pickup trucks. He was the only white person there and everyone in the place had guns. Pulling a drink from a cooler, he headed to the cash register. The guy behind the register pulled what appeared to be a .44 magnum, started cussing, then ran to the gas pumps. Someone had just pumped gas and drove away without paying. The thing he hated about leaving the place was walking by the best-looking biscuits and gravy he had ever seen.

He proceeded on the narrow road to a small railroad overpass with a passage just large enough for his wrecker truck. He was thinking someone could pull a car in front of that and block him from leaving. There was an old station wagon sitting there with an even older man scratching his head, looking at a flat tire. Gene stopped to help the old fellow change the tire. While changing it, he saw a woman on the front seat in a slumped over position. He asked if she was okay and was told she was dead. After tightening the lug bolts he dropped the car to see if she would move. She didn't move. The old fellow said he was taking her to a nearby hospital. This was the last straw.

Gene turned around and headed home!

KINDERGARTEN KID

An agreement was made between a mother and the principal of an elementary school regarding the mother's kindergarten student. The mother owned a shop in Charleston, West Virginia, and had to drop her son off very early. The principal was there early each day and agreed to take the boy along as she inspected the school. New floor tiles were being installed in the cafeteria. A few of the tiles were faded and had to be replaced. An employee of the flooring company came in over the weekend and marked X's on each tile that needed to be replaced. When inspecting the school on Monday morning, the young student said, "I guess the fellow playing the O's didn't show up."

The student was in kindergarten with a sixth-grade reading level. On his first day in school he saw the "Pull" lever written on the fire alarm and, of course, pulled.

JEAN RUNNERS

A good friend of mine, Jean Kennedy, was the principal of an elementary school in Pinch, West Virginia. The school had around one thousand students with a staff of maybe eighty to one hundred. The grades were from preschool through sixth grade. There were also classes for learning disabled and physically handicapped. The school had a single road passing it with one direction going by a church and the other to a "Y" in the road. The staff was male and female, ranging in age from young to retirement age. One young female teacher, Cecilia, was very disciplined and ran a few miles each day to stay in shape. This was important, as every now and then a kindergarten or leaning disabled student would run out the door and head for home as fast as they could run. The principal would notify Cecilia, "Runner Church" or "Runner Y", giving her the direction. There was an assistant in her classroom, enabling her to take off in a moment's notice. The principal kept her car parked with the front facing out for a quicker exit. The plan was such a success that no students ever made it past the end of school property.

BAR ROOM DENTIST

The story begins as Ron, an old high school friend, was going home from work one afternoon and stopped in a local bar. His reason for stopping was that they had a pool table. Now my friend had spent a large portion of his teenage years in a local pool room. In the many hours spent there he became quite skilled at the game. In these bars I have heard that sometimes they gamble a little. I'm sure my friend never considered this possibility.

It was a little early and Ron was the only customer there, so he sat down and ordered a beer. About that time another customer came in, sat down, and started complaining about a sore tooth. When asked by the bartender why he didn't have it pulled, he said he could not afford a dentist. The bartender said it wasn't a problem as he could pull the tooth for him. The customer said, "You're crazy! There is no way I would let you try that!"

The bartender, a little offended, asked who he thought pulled the teeth of all the hunting dogs out back. As the discussion went on, a bottle of bourbon was produced, and a few shots were downed. After half an hour of discussion went on which included enough booze to alter the courage level, the bartender went out to his pickup truck and brought in a rusty pair of channel locks. He pinned the customer down with his knees and began the loud struggle. Within a couple of minutes, the bloody tooth was held up in the rusty channel locks. The procedure was followed with a few more shots for numbing and medicinal purposes. Ron had lost his interest in pool and left for home.

BIG DAVY & ELECTRONIC CHICKEN

When my first marriage came to an end my children and I moved into a house with little or nothing. The children had their bedroom furniture and in by bedroom was a desk, file cabinet, set of weights, and a lawn recliner. The worst part was there was very little in the kitchen. We went to a local discount store and bought some plastic dishes and silverware that would bend with very little pressure. We also bought one frying pan and a couple of bowls and thought we were ready. We never planned our meals and would open the refrigerator when it was time to eat. One evening we pulled a chicken out of the freezer and decided it would be our dinner. It was frozen solid, so we put it in the microwave thinking it was on defrost. After about 15 minutes we remembered it was in there and removed it. The chicken was fully cooked, and the skin was a light gray. It didn't smell so good, either. We then decided to light a charcoal grill that someone had left in the back yard, thinking we would change the color and smell to something more palatable. We were very hungry and didn't let the charcoal burn long enough. After a few minutes on the grill the chicken did have a better color but tasted like lighter fluid. The name for that dish became electronic chicken.

Our toaster was one that I had repaired. My ex-wife hand made a terry cloth cover for it and it was a little tight. When she put it on the toaster it turned on the toaster. The toaster heated up and caught the cover on fire, filling the toaster with burnt terry cloth. No problem. I took it apart, cleaned it, and reassembled it. People from West Virginia do not purchase new things, we repair what we have. In the assembly I must have missed something, because after my repair any toast we made would pop up and fly completely out onto the counter. When toasting one piece of toast it was thrown for quite a distance. We noticed that if we toasted a single slice it would always land in the same place, so we began setting a plate there to catch it. Whenever we had guests we amazed them by making toast and catching it in a plate as if it was an ordinary thing.

During this time there was a mentally handicapped fellow that worked as a dish washer down the street from my office. Each day after work he would walk up to my store for a ride home. This ride was important to him as he weighed three hundred and eighty pounds and had to walk quite a distance to the bus.

Regular scales don't register weight that high, so he was weighed using truck scales. A car was placed on truck scales by itself. He was then placed in the car, to determine his weight.

He had attended a state school for several years where he was taught to live in a strict routine which he really took to heart. He met a retarded girl at the school and married her. Being mentally handicapped he held a job, was married, and led a pretty good life.

On the way home, I would ask him what he was fixing for dinner, as he was the cook for himself and his wife. His training had him pre-planning his meals and having everything ready for his return home. The meal included protein, green vegetables, and a carbohydrate. Also included was a little dessert. My business was marketing and servicing complicated office equipment and I'm supposed to be the smart guy, but he was way ahead of me as I had no clue what we were having. When asked if he knew how to prepare electronic chicken I was clearly ahead on that.

INSURANCE SALESMAN

One rainy, dreary day while in my shop doing paperwork, an insurance man walked in canvassing. I was in a rotten mood that day, and certainly wasn't interested in his pitch. These guys go through training and are drilled on the idea that the more people you talk to the greater your success. Don't be discouraged by the No's because they lead to a Yes. Use the prospective customer's name over and over and they love it. Ask as many questions as possible with obvious Yes answers because they are more likely to say Yes. This salesman had obviously been canvassing in the rain, as his glasses were covered by rain drops and his hair was soaked. I was also irritated by the fact that insurance men only need a sheet of paper to make a sale while I must buy, stock, and deliver merchandise.

I told the salesman, "I'll tell you want I can do for you. For $50 a month, if your dog dies we will crap in your yard, howl at the moon and dig holes everywhere. If your mother-in-law dies, we will call every other night for two months to tell you what a low-down son of a bitch you are. If you break your left arm we will give you $150. If your break your other arm we will break a leg for free." I went on like that for a while and stopped for a second. He looked at me and said that he had been canvassing all day and we were the only ones that had been nice to him.

At that point I felt sorry for him, but still bought no insurance.

COMPETITORS

When opening my business in Fairfax, Virginia, I had three major competitors. One was located in Alexandria and the other was a partnership with offices in Vienna and Falls Church. As our business grew, we picked up Fairfax County as an account, which infuriated the fellow in Alexandria, as he had previously been selling to them. The owner there was a German who ran away from home at thirteen years of age and grew up working on fishing boats out of Atlantic City. To say he was a hard-nosed character would be an understatement. He hated my guts!

About once a month, a young fellow would walk in looking for a delivery driver position. When he was offered a job with a friend who had a moving business, he loudly declined, saying he only wanted a job as a delivery driver. It became apparent that he was only going around once a month to gather names from businesses and continue collecting unemployment money. The light bulb came on and I sent him to my competitor in Alexandria. I gave the fellow my business card and told him that the competitor in Alexandria was a close friend. Then I instructed him on how to mispronounce his name. That afternoon my young friend called back to tell me there had been a mistake, there was no job opening there, and that my competitor really did not like me.

One afternoon my secretary and a couple of technicians came back to tell me there was a crazy woman up front in the showroom causing a commotion and cursing them. I walked up front to see how I could help and saw her car parked facing the wrong direction on the one-way street in a No Parking Zone. I knew what they told me was right. An angry faced woman was there, and I greeted her with a smile and asked how I could be of assistance. After she uttered a few incoherent sentences she was informed that we did not have what she wanted, but a competitor in Vienna specialized in her interest. I very carefully drew a map for her and gave her my card for presentation upon arrival at the store in Vienna.

The partnership between the two stores broke up, a very bitter situation. Every now and then I would stop in to the competitors' stores for a supply item, part, or some small item. When in the Vienna store I would complement the owner for helping me and mention my surprise at being treated this nicely because his ex-partner had said the week before that he was an asshole. This would result in a five-minute tirade. When in Falls Church I would do the same thing.

SMOKING AFTER

My wife and I, along with several other couples, were invited to the home of a couple that had recently sold a computer business for several million dollars. After the sale, they constructed a lavish home in McLean, Virginia. The area is one of the most exclusive in the Washington, D.C., metro area. This is an area where land is sold by the square foot instead of the acre like in a downtown office building area. The home was quite large and imposing. After completion, a ballroom costing over a million dollars was added and used not only for the family, but also local organizations for benefits and similar activities.

Our group was given a tour of the home which included three floors and a completed basement. These areas were filled with all sorts of articles ranging from slot machines, giant vases, numerous paintings, lamps, massive furniture and musical instruments.

After returning home, our group sat down for dinner and began discussing what we had seen. One of the women asked, "Did you see that picture coming down the stairs?" It was a naked woman lying back with a cloud coming up between her legs. I said, "I'm surprised that you are not familiar with that, it's famous the world over! It's called Smoking after Sex!"

DEB WORKOUT QUESTION

Several friends and I met in Manassas, Virginia, to work out three times a week. After returning home, my wife would ask, "What did you talk about?" She and the wives of the group had decided at one point to work out at the same time and come along with us. The women never really got into the workouts, and mostly stood around talking to each other. After a few visits to the gym they stopped coming.

They, of course, observed our constant and active conversations. Our conversations consisted of remarks to each other, jokes, and in guy fashion, nothing of any substance. Not really things you would remember and report after the workouts. The group, including wives, socialized, going to movies, dinners, etc.

When returning home, my wife would ask if we discussed going to the movies, what everyone will be wearing, are we going out to dinner, and questions about our social life. I, of course, told her that I remembered nothing. After several weeks of being asked what we had talked about I promised her that I would pay attention to the night's conversations and give her a report. When I returned home that night, after paying attention to our conversations, I was ready to report.

Me: "Tonight we talked about farting in elevators."

Wife: "What? You spent the whole evening talking about farting in elevators?"

Me: "You have to realize that it's a very complicated science, honey, and requires planning. There is a lot more to it than stepping on the elevator and blasting off. If you ease out a silent fart you must look innocent or ask loudly who farted. If you fart loudly a look of disgust must be aimed at a nearby passenger. A loud fart is commonly referred to as a cheek flapper. Another tactic is to fart loudly as the elevator doors are opening, and you are stepping off, leaving the remaining passengers with the aromatic deposit. This is called the parting shot."

She never asked about our conversations again.

CLICK CREPES

I met a fellow in Sterling, Virginia, who was a teacher in Fairfax County Schools. In addition, he owned a local used car lot. At the time I was selling office equipment to the school board and rebuilding and selling used cars on the side. We became close friends as our interests were so similar and he had a great sense of humor as well. Our wives had never met so we decided to go out to dinner at a local restaurant the next Saturday night. His wife was a librarian for Fairfax County Schools and a very proper person, unlike John or me. His wife selected a French restaurant for our dinner and introduction. We met there one evening, introduced the wives, and were seated. In checking the menu for escargot, we found it was not listed. I said to the waiter, "I see you have snails." With a concerned and questioning look on his face, he asked where they were listed on the menu. My answer was, "Right here, it says 'Creeps'." Of course, it said crepes. John was laughing as the wives tried to hide. The waiter, trying not to laugh, explained the difference. It was our policy to embarrass the wives at least once in every restaurant.

TAKING THE WIVES TO A NICE RESTAURANT

My wife had wanted to go to the Inn at Little Washington for some time, and on a special occasion we went out there. The restaurant was absolutely one of the top-rated places on the East coast, and the choice of stars and celebrities who come to the Washington, D.C., metro area. The cost at that time for a dinner for two was well over four hundred dollars. In keeping with its status, it was completely over decorated.

As we entered, I said to my wife, "Look honey, they wallpapered the ceiling." This remark drew some curious looks from the other patrons and was completely ignored by my wife. The wait staff is choreographed. If there are four people seated at a table, four waiters simultaneously, with a flourish, set the plates in front of each patron at the same time.

For dessert I had ice cream and caramel, which was served in a bowl tilted in my direction. I notified the waiter that my bowl was crooked, to which he replied that it was for my convenience. I told him it looked like a factory defect.

Between each serving, a small spoon of sorbet is served to cleanse the palette. When asked if everything was satisfactory, a friend of mine replied, "I would like some more of that ice cream."

In Great Falls, Virginia, is an upscale restaurant called Chez Francois. A wonderful place and everything is as close to perfect as humanly possible. One evening I commented to a waiter on the impeccable quality of the decor for which he thanked me. I then asked if it had ever been a Mexican restaurant. He walked away.

TRICO TECHNICIAN

When calling back to my office one afternoon, I was told there had been a fight between two employees, one male and one female. Oh, NO! All kinds of scenarios began running through my mind. Were the police called? Who do I fire? Was either injured? What will happen when the husband finds out? If I don't fire one of them they can't be there without supervision.

When asking whether the female was injured, I was told it was the other way around. The male involved kept most of my employees mad with his derogatory remarks, and it wasn't surprising he was involved. The infraction occurred when he told the rather large secretary that she was fat. She chased him all over the office, breaking chairs and tables, and hitting him with anything available. The reaction of the husband when hearing what happened was, "It serves him right." He knew what she was capable of first hand and had no reason to be mad.

It took three days to reassemble the office. She had beaten the hell out of him. I asked him back to my office and we had a little discussion regarding his conversations with others. He was told that everybody says things that offend others. Unfortunately, I do the same, but making somebody mad is rare and unintentional. I told him that if he talked to ten people, at least nine of them would be offended. Therefore, there has to be some intent involved on his part.

He reluctantly agreed.

OLD PEOPLE FARTS

As you go through life you see various things happening and, as they do, you come up with theories to explain the events. Our subject is old people's farts. When watching an old person getting up and walking across the room you might hear a "poot, poot, poot," or a walking fart. The next category is the phantom, as you hear nothing but are engulfed by a deadly smell while the older person goes about their tasks and says nothing. Another category is the cheek flapper, which usually happens when they bend over. In this category they blast off and once again say nothing.

I had a few theories to explain this phenomenon. The first is they don't really know it's happening. The second is they had lost all control along with poor hearing and loss of ability to smell. As a result of the previously mentioned conditions they of course were not embarrassed. While shopping with my wife recently I was standing a few steps behind her as she checked out. Having accumulated a large quantity of gas, I cut loose with a loud fart. Presently I am seventy-eight, and quite healthy. I can hear, smell, and have feeling in the subject area. I am fully aware of my actions. I came to the realization that old people know exactly what they are doing, but no longer give a shit.

HI YO

The youngest daughter of a great friend that I grew up with in the big city of Dunbar had married a fellow whose last name was Silber. She became pregnant and my friend Bill was looking forward to a new granddaughter. The family was looking for a name and, as usual, I had some suggestions. My first suggestion was, "Why not call her Hi Yo, as in Hi Yo Silber?" My second was if she became an athlete and could run about quick, she could be called Quick Silber. My third was if she was very good, call her Sterling Silber. Unfortunately, my ideas where met with a frown and totally rejected. To Bill, she is a beautiful young lady and I know you are very proud of her, as you should be. I apologize for including this in the book.

PONTIAC JUDGE

While living in Northern Virginia a number of people I grew up with lived there as well. Years earlier in Dunbar, the fellow next door moved in at the age of four and we became buddies. Unfortunately, our parents were not happy with the friendship and did not want us to play together, which was partially successful. There were four of us from a one-block area of 20th Street and another from 21st Street who eventually ended up in Northern Virginia. The fellow next door and I were both drummers in the Dunbar High School Marching Band, marching side by side. After moving on in life, he owned a salvage pool for wrecked, stolen or damaged cars in Centreville, Virginia. My friend from 21st Street became an attorney and had a law firm in Manassas. I had gone into the office equipment business and had a location in Manassas. The attorney had a classmate who became an attorney at his firm and later on became a judge.

The classmate, unlike the three of us, was very serious and not really into our kind of humor. He had just purchased a new Pontiac. The four of us prominent businessmen were going for lunch and a test drive. While attempting to pull away from a parking place this judge was blocked by two elderly women attempting to get into the car in front of us. Getting in the car was made difficult by the fact one of them was on crutches. As we were waiting for the women to clear the way, I reached over and blew the horn. Our driver was mortified, and the women gave him a look of angry disbelief. This was a very common thing to do in Dunbar, to the extent that my horn button was installed under the carpet by the brake pedal for purposes of prevention.

My buddies in the back seat were laughing quite loudly.

MANASSAS HOSPITAL

A group of friends including an attorney, a prosecuting attorney, judge, high school coach, IBM sales representative, and myself, would meet at 6:30 in the morning each Saturday. After working out for a little over an hour we would go to the Manassas Hospital for a healthy breakfast. The breakfast usually consisted of hard-boiled eggs, oatmeal, fruit, etc. The selection was quite large, and the food was always very good. In addition, the prices were also very reasonable. Conversations at the table were animated and a little loud at times, making the breakfast even more enjoyable. For some reason the Hospital stopped making oatmeal and substituted it with Cream of Wheat. We asked the employees at the cash register and the food preppers why the change had been made. We never got a satisfactory answer. On the wall was a suggestion box, so we presented our complaint. This resulted in no change. The prosecuting attorney was a young lady who didn't attend on a regular basis. We told her that we used her name on the complaints we submitted thinking it would have a greater impact.

She was then told the complaints using her name had been using the "F" word to enhance her pleas. For some reason she objected to our using her name. One Saturday we were all there and she even brought her brother, as he was visiting. We went over to the cashier, informed her of what had been going on, and asked her to come to our table and speak to the young lady. The register operator could have won an academy award for her performance. She approached the table with an indignant look on her face and asked if there was a Nancy Grace at the table. Nancy (not her name), with a look of surprise and apprehension, said, "Yes, that's me." The cashier said to her with an indignant voice, "We happen to like our cream of wheat and think it's good for you." She then spun around and stomped away. Nancy's mouth was wide in amazement until we started laughing, whereupon she began throwing things at us.

MANASSAS GARAGE

A garage in Manassas, Virginia, had been displaced by road improvements. A parking lot was being constructed behind a new building. The lot had trees, brush, trash, and various other things to be cleared before being covered by gravel. While clearing the lot, they found a 15" rubber dildo which was taken inside. A cousin of the owner had his pickup truck in for repair, and without his knowledge the dildo was wired to the front of the truck, sticking out forward. The truck was parked with the front up against the fence, so the driver was not aware of what was on the grill.

As the driver drove the truck home, he noticed people laughing but really didn't think much about it. When he arrived at home and went in he was none the wiser. He became aware of it when neighborhood children were laughing and hitting it with a stick, watching it bounce and of course the guys at the garage knew nothing about it. It was impossible to enter the garage and not laugh. In the front of the garage was a sign, "If it has tires or tits you will have trouble with it."

LIQUOR LICENSE

An attorney in Manassas, Virginia, was visited in his office by two young ladies. They had been to the courthouse seeking a marriage license and were very disappointed to hear that same sex marriage was illegal in the state of Virginia. Not to be denied, they inquired about ways of handling the situation. In talking to people in the legal profession, they were referred to the attorney known to be creative and very diligent in working in the interest of his clients. Upon being presented with the dilemma, the attorney asked for a couple of days to research the question. He consulted with colleagues, got on his computer and did research, and came to a conclusion for a solution. When the two ladies were asked to return and were very excited when they were told he thought he could help them. They were given a document and asked to take their time and read through it. They were also instructed that if there were any questions to please ask. The ladies were delighted with the approach and thanked him. After signing the document, having it notarized, and writing a check to the attorney, they departed very happily with their liquor (Licker) license.

This terrible sexist story may not be true.

LARRY

A friend who went to work for me as a salesman had grown up in Pennsboro, West Virginia. He ran away from home in the sixth grade and went no further in school. He had musical talent and struggled to make it by playing his guitar and singing in bars. He then joined the Marine Corp. He was drunk when he joined and had the impression they would be gone for a weekend. When arriving at Paris Island, being lined up and called a shit maggot, he realized he may be there for a while.

He had a mop of hair when he arrived at boot camp. He was asked how he would like it cut and said to just take a little off the sides. The barber smiled and ran the razor straight through the middle and cut it all off. He was rather bull-headed and was recycled through basic training three times. When enlisting he weighed one hundred twenty-five pounds, and after the third time through basic he weighed one hundred seventy five pounds. On the third time through, he thought that if he didn't straighten up they would kill him. Back then they would smack you around.

Larry has been squared away, dressing properly and performing the tasks in life to the best of his ability. He is still a Marine in spirit. He married a girl from home and moved into an apartment off base. Neither of them knew how to cook. One morning, while cooking breakfast, the skillet caught on fire. Larry panicked and instead of covering the skillet to smother the flames, he opened a window and threw the skillet out. They lived on the third floor of an apartment building and had large pine trees lining the building. The trees erupted in flames. Larry closed the window and pretended to know nothing.

After befriending a fellow Marine, Larry invited the Marine and his wife over for dinner. His guest was from New York and knew nothing of West Virginia cuisine. He was served squirrel, pickled corn and a few more delicacies. His fellow Marine returned to base and swore Larry was trying to poison him.

Larry went to work for me as a salesman and did an extremely good job. He became my sales manager and was with me for over twenty years. The customers loved him and his West Virginia twang. We sold one of the first electronic cash registers to a local VFW Post in Annandale, Virginia. The register began having some problems and the customer wanted help NOW. The only person near there at the time was Larry. He was a salesman and knew nothing about technical issues. We asked Larry to stop by to see what was wrong in the hope he would get lucky and solve the problem. Sitting at the bar directly in front of the register was a fellow who had been drinking and was plastered. As Larry started checking the register, the drunk started saying, "Get him out of here, he doesn't know what he's doing!" Of course, this was true. That is the maddest I ever saw Larry.

An employee came in with his dog one day, and it was the skinniest, worst looking dog I've ever seen. Larry looked at it and asked, "What is that?" I recognized the dog as a Whippet and told Larry what it was. He had never heard of a Whippet and thought I had just made up a name. I added, "The dogs are so useless the only thing you can do is Whip It."

SUNDRA

Next door to my business there was a print shop. A very nice, soft-spoken gentleman owned the business and conducted it in a dignified manner, unlike his neighbor. Around the corner there was a real estate office. We were all on a first name basis. The owner of the real estate office was walking down Main Street and encountered two stray dogs wandering around. He decided it was his civic and humane duty to catch the dogs and place them where they could be picked up later by the proper authorities. He caught the dogs and took them into the print shop for them to hold until the dog catcher arrived. Of course, his office was right around the corner, but he selected the print shop. The dog catcher took about three hours (or longer) to arrive. In that time, the dogs were howling and barking and crapped in the floor. Joe, the print shop owner, returned after a couple of hours and was furious.

The back of our shop had a common door to both shops, which gave us an idea. Whenever we saw a stray animal on Main Street, we would catch it and send it through Joe's back door. The animals would see the front door and go trotting to the front, right by Joe's desk. He became used to it over a period of time.

Down Main Street, a Hay and Grain store closed down and the owners were trying to sell the building, so they left a fellow there to show the property and keep an eye on the place. Between Main Street and the parking lot to the rear there was a connecting driveway going by their loading dock. The fellow watching the building would come out to watch us go by even though we passed through there for over twelve years. He even made a remark or two about our passing through. We decided to take action. We cleared some of the information from a parking ticket issued in the rear lot. Using whiteout, we removed the officer's name, badge number, date, and offenses. We made a copy of the ticket and filled it in as follows: The officer's name on the new ticket was Tasso (the name of the fellow who owned the restaurant next door), his badge number was "007". We check marked every offense listed on the ticket. In order to place the ticket on this man's windshield we needed to distract him. Luckily someone came by to look at the inside of the building. We placed the ticket while walking to the parking lot. We were sure he would look at the ticket and realize it was a joke.

When the man saw the ticket on his truck he screamed, jumped into the truck, and spun out for the City Hall. We later learned he ran into the Chief of Police's office, threw the ticket down and continued to scream. The chief picked up the ticket to read and was soon joined by two more officers. The chief began to smile, and started laughing, along with the other officers. When he realized he was had, he grabbed the ticket and left as the officers laughed him out the door.

For the rest of the week he went up and down Main Street asking if anybody knew about the ticket. I stopped him and, of course, said I knew nothing about it, but it appeared to be a Xerox copy and the only person on the street with a Xerox copier was Joe at the Print Shop.

Our building fronted on Main Street in Fairfax City, with four separate businesses located there. Mine was office equipment, Joe's print shop, a bank, and Susan's store selling knickknacks. Susan was a bubbly, overly emotional person always coming in with less-that-worthwhile business ideas. One day Susan came in wanting the four businesses there to each buy a planter with flowers to place in the front of each store. The price was $25.00 each. Her thought was that it would be beneficial as it would draw much attention to our businesses. I gave her $25, as did the bank, but Joe at the print shop thought it was stupid and refused. Susan brought in the planters and placed in front of our stores (except for the print shop). After a couple of weeks, one day at 5:00 we were all leaving for the day. Susan had gone home early, and Joe was out on calls. We took all three flower pots and locked them in Joe's front showroom. The next morning, she rushed through our door saying the planters were gone. I went out front to help her look for them and exclaimed, "There they are in Joe's office!" Joe opened a little later than we did, so she could not retrieve them at the time. After Joe arrived, she went stomping over to his office and we could hear her screaming through the wall. She later exclaimed that he was jealous.

TYPEWRITER PSYCHIATRIST

When servicing Royal typewriters, we would encounter situations where repairing the machine would not fix the problem. In some cases, in order to facilitate a repair, the typist must be fixed. Before the computer took over and appeared on every desk, they all had typewriters. Large organizations had typing pools. These were usually in a large room with the typists in rows with the supervisor in a position to view the activity. I was dispatched to a typing pool for the West Virginia Supreme Court in Charleston. When walking in, I saw about twenty typists with a rather large older lady seated in the middle. The look on her face indicated something just wasn't right. It was kind of like she smelled something bad. When approaching her, I noticed the typists looking at me cautiously with slight smiles out of the corners of their eyes. The problem was with the large supervisor's machine. She placed a piece of paper in the typewriter and started typing. The problem became obvious as her timing was bad, and she classed the type bars together. The look on her face told me that telling her she was the problem would not end well. I pretended to service the typewriter, removing the side panels, lubricating areas and typing a sample sheet. I stopped and asked her a question. *"How long have you been doing this job?"* Her answer was over forty-five years. I said to her that in all those years her speed had increased to the point that she was too fast for the typewriter and the only solution was for her to slow down. After saying this, I glanced at the other typists and saw them raising their eyebrows with a look of disappointment, as they were expecting me to tell her that she was the problem. She smiled broadly and asked me if I would like a cup of coffee.

All attempts to solve customer problems were not successful. A young technician was called to an office and told the Royal Electric typewriter was too loud, much louder that the IBM. The typewriters were on two desks side by side. The complaining customer was asked to stand in the center between the two. She was then asked which one was the loudest, to which she answered the Royal. She was then asked to move closer to the IBM and asked again. Her answer, again, was that the Royal was the loudest. Then our technician said, "Ok, now I will turn on the Royal." It had not been running. Several people in the office laughed while the operator threw our technician out of the office. He had won the argument but could never return.

GROWING OLDER SIGNS

When I reached the age of fifty I started receiving AARP mailers. When checking the address, I could not believe it was addressed to me. What in the hell is this?

A friend who has exercised on a regular basis for years and even run twenty-six-mile marathons, when going to his doctor, was asked these questions: *Can you brush your own teeth? Can you get up out of a chair on your own without help? Can you hold your urine all the way to the commode?* The look of complete disgust on his face caused the doctor to lay the question list down and say that was a new government requirement.

When going to the pharmacy recently I was asked for my date of birth. Upon giving them the date, the young lady got a big smile on her face and said she had something I would like. She came back with a flip top lid for the prescription bottle instead of the childproof lid, certain I would think it was great. After telling her I didn't care, either type was okay, she seemed disappointed.

A few months ago, I received a notice announcing my sixtieth high school reunion. The entire sheet was written in capital letters about a quarter of an inch tall. When asked about the print size, the lady who sent out the notice said the letter size was because she didn't know how to operate her computer and that was all she could do. This was even worse than my first thought.

People of my age have changed the subject of our conversations almost entirely to health problems, doctors, medicines, procedures, and "Oh, I feel bad." My friend that exercises, not being the victim of all these ailments, joins the conversation by telling everybody about fake ailments. We talk mostly about our hemorrhoids, which neither of us have. I threw in a painful story of my hemorrhoid being caught in the back wheel of a bicycle the previous week. That is an example of our contribution to this subject.

WITCH DOCTOR

While attending a church in Sterling, VA, I became acquainted with a fellow who had a great sense of humor and we became friends. He worked for the Federal Government as a purchasing agent and I sold office equipment. He did buy some equipment from me. Our business meetings consisted of five minutes of business and thirty minutes of jokes and laughing. In that type of business relationship, I never needed an appointment. The years passed, and he retired and moved to Tennessee, where he had grown up and had several brothers. He was a devout Christian and he and his wife felt led to go to the mission field. They spent five years serving in South Africa for the Southern Baptist Convention. While serving, his health took a downward turn and he was given a few prescriptions. When the five years ended he returned to the USA and began the process of finding a house and reestablishing his life here. In phone conversations I became aware of his efforts to find a house and a few more things. It seems that the terminology used on prescriptions in South Africa is different than that used here in the USA. The light bulb came on and I conspired with a friend who has a real gift of gab. He called pretending to be with the Food and Drug Administration, using the following spiel:

I am with the FDA and we understand you recently returned after serving for five years in South Africa. We would like to thank you for your service and give you some assistance with your prescriptions. As you know, South African terminology is quite different than ours, as is their medical system. Our agent that covers that area is here with me and will take over the phone call in a few seconds. He will be a little difficult to understand due to his native language, so I have asked him to take it a little slower than usual. Actually, he is a witch doctor, and of course we discussed the many differences in our two systems.

My Tennessee friend's answer was, "Witch doctor? Who is this?" The caller than says, "Mr. Smith (not his name), you of all people should understand these extreme differences."

He hung up the phone and called me, asking me to stop these yahoos from calling him, and I did. I already had an attorney buddy who, at one time, had a real estate title company. He was to tell him he was from HUD and had been cheated on his mortgage.

TELEMARKETER CALLS

I love taking telephone calls from telemarketers or people with a wrong number. Telemarketers who engage you on a one-to-one basis trying to sell something or scam you are my favorites.

Scenario 1)
Ring

- Caller: *Hello, Is Mary there?*
- Me: *Yes, she is, but I don't think we can get her to the phone. She's been drinking.*

Scenario 2)
Ring

- Caller: *Hello, Is Mary there?*
- Me: *You just missed her. She left with her boyfriend five minutes ago.*

Scenario 3)
Ring

- Caller: Hello, I am with so-and-so Insurance Company, and we are offering a two hundred fifty-thousand-dollar policy for twenty dollars a month. This would be a wonderful investment for your family and show them your loyalty and love.
- Me: That sounds great and that is an unbelievable price, what a deal! I would buy that for sure, but my attorney says that it isn't safe for a married man to be worth more dead than alive. The life expectancy is around six months!

Scenario 4)
Ring

- Caller: *(Strong accent) Hello, I am work with your Windows. Go to your Windows.*
- Me: *It's raining, and we have them closed.*
- Caller: *Go to Windows.*
- Me: *We just rent here and if they break the landlord fixes them.*
- Caller: *Windows on Screen.*
- Me: *its winter here and we don't have any bugs now.*

- Caller: *(Getting angry) It's your computer, Mother Fxxxxr (and hangs up)*

Scenario 5)

During a visit to the home of a friend whose last name is Blais, a call from a magazine sales company came in. The Caller ID appeared on the TV screen and we knew it was a telemarketer. My friend said he wasn't going to take the call as he didn't want to be bothered so I volunteered to take it.

Ring

- Caller: *Hello, is Mr. Blais there?*
- Me: *How did you get that name?*
- Caller: *From a list of previous customers.*
- Me: *I ask because Blais is an alias and not his real name. Blais is his stage name, used in several movies he has made. His most successful movie was Dennis Does Dallas – Gay Porn. I bet you saw that one. His real name is John Wayne, He entered the movie business using that name, but it didn't work in the movies because he has a hair lip. In a western movie he had to say "Shtick 'em up partner." His voice just didn't cast that strong western image.*
- Caller: *(Hangs up)*

CAR LOT

In the process of restoring the building used for my car lot in Winchester Virginia, several of the locals were hired for various jobs. The young gentlemen were what is known as rednecks. Now a redneck will work hard, sweat, call in friends when help is needed, and do an excellent job. The weakness, however, came if you pissed them off. They had all been employed by other businesses in previous years and had experience in plumbing, electrical, AC, construction, concrete, and could do anything. They would work for varied amounts of time until difficulties would arise. Difficulties like being unexpectedly gone for a week of time hunting, an extended drunken hangover, showing up drunk for work, and time off for court and/or time served.

The building was square with the roof shaped like a pyramid. The shingles were fake barrel tile made of metal. A fellow was on the roof painting, using a thick coating to prevent leaks, and changing the color to black as the base was white. It was summer, and several of the hot tiles had cracks underneath, a few with bees' nests. The worker on top had bees swirling all around him. I noticed he was biting his tongue, so I asked him why. He said his daddy told him that bees can't sting you when you bite your tongue. He was probably nine years old when his dad said that to him, and now he was forty.

A friend owned a junk yard close by and had a part time worker they all called "Fat Boy." In wanting to hire Fat Boy to do some mechanical work, I asked for his name and phone number. It took about two days, as nobody had any idea what his real name was. When calling the number, I asked to speak to Norman (which I finally learned was his name) because it didn't seem right to ask for Fat Boy. He wasn't really fat. The phone was answered by a lady who quickly asked who was calling. After explaining that I wanted to hire him to work at the car lot, she very loudly called, "Hey Fat Boy!"

A fellow named Junior purchased a Chevrolet Blazer and we financed the transaction. He had an eye that looked right and the other eye kind of wandered around in no particular direction. His good eye was the one that pointed right, so he would turn his head sideways to complete paperwork. If asked how he was doing, he would give a half hour lecture starting with, "The world is going to hell on a jet plane ..." I made that mistake twice.

Another worker, named Festus, asked me to buy a truck for him as payment for his services. On route 50 just outside of town there was an old short bed

Chevrolet with a price tag of 450.00. Festus had done a number of things at the lot and was owed a greater figure, so we made the deal. About a month later he came in the office wearing a sport shirt and casual pants instead of the Army surplus garb he usually wore. I asked him if he had been preaching at a local church as he looked so good. His reply was that he was returning from court. He had been arrested for going one hundred and ten miles per hour down Valley Avenue. By the way, Valley Avenue is a main drag and goes by the Mall, Lowes, restaurants and generally has a lot of traffic. I asked him why he was going so fast and what he was driving. He was driving the pickup truck he got from me and of course he was told if I knew it was that fast it would have cost more. He said he was trying it out after submerging it in the Shenandoah River. There is a low water bridge just above the river surface when the water is at normal level that goes under water as the river rises. He was drinking with some friends and decided to show off by crossing in deep water. Before starting across he uttered the famous redneck saying, "Watch this". About half way across he was swept off the bridge. A friend with a wrecker pulled it out the next day and the repair was made. He had walked out of court, as the radar gun had not been calibrated. As he did he made he made a less than nice remark to the police officer, probably causing another problem at a later date. I sold the cheapest cars in town and did not serve the intelligencia.

My wife worked at the car lot doing the books and taking payments. They all called her my "Old Lady", which she wasn't crazy about. They also called her "Large and In Charge". She only liked half of that name.

One Saturday four people walked onto the lot from different directions. While showing cars I realized they were all on a first name basis, which meant if you dealt poorly with one everyone in Winchester would know.

Another fellow came on the lot several times looking at cars. He never bought but always had stories to tell. Don't know if he was stupid or thought I was. He supposedly bought some acreage outside town and paid for it by selling the snakes the caught. One hundred ten thousand dollars cash for the rattlesnakes and copperheads. He said his friend had a pen full of pigs, including a mama pig and a bunch of little ones. It seems some of the piglets were getting sick and a couple died. After calling the vet he was asked if he had killed a snake recently. He answered, "Yes, it's hanging over the fence over there." The dead snake was a racer, which was something the vet expected. According to the story, the racer snake will begin to nurse on the mama pig and, if killed, the piglets would get sick. In addition, the racer will chase you and adjust its speed to yours. The faster you go the faster the snake goes until it trips you. Since a racer is non-poisonous and not really large I have no clue what it does once you are down. Come to think of it, all his stories were about snakes.

FOOT FETISH

A few years ago in the small town of New Smyrna Beach, Florida, there was a fellow who would appear in the bedrooms of women who were sleeping. No real damage was done to the doors or windows on entry. I do not recall any mention of weapons or the women being threatened. In addition, none of the women were injured. Upon uncovering the feet of his victims, he probably woke them up. He had a foot fetish and would begin doing whatever people with that fetish do. The women with clean feet got extra attention. The attacker was completely nude and had nothing covering his face. Strangely enough, he was never arrested, as not a single woman could describe his face. He was never apprehended, as police had nothing to give them direction.

My wife and I were with a group of friends discussing the matter and questioning what people with a foot fetish do. Is it feet only? How long does this last? One foot at a time?

One woman in the group commented that I must not have a foot fetish, as my wife knew so little about the act. My comment was that I have higher aspirations.

JOE

My older brother Joe had always wanted to become a doctor, and with his wife working, the GI bill, and student debt, he succeeded. He was a very calm man that thought things out and was very deliberate in his approach to life. A couple of years ago Joe passed away. At his funeral several of his colleagues remarked about his demeanor and how much they valued his advice. He was well read and could speak on just about any subject with some depth of knowledge. I think he read more books in a month than I have read in a lifetime.

His son-in-laws reminisced about conversations they had about star constellations and groupings, birds, and life in general. The day he passed away he called all three of his daughters to tell them he loved them, as if he knew what was going to happen. His wife was devastated, and the family was quite concerned about her ability to cope in the future.

Since then, the family has found fresh red roses placed at his grave. They have no idea who placed them there.

My frequent telephone conversations with Joe were usually while he was in his car waiting for his wife, who was shopping.

My youngest daughter and my son were with me during Joe's funeral service. Even though I know for sure he is in a better place, a few audible sobs slipped out, like those from his wife, daughters, and even the sons-in-law. My daughter supplied me with a couple of tissues, which I filled with tears and a little snot. The service was held in a large Catholic church. On our way out of the sanctuary I began looking for a trash can for the used tissues. There was a receptacle on the back wall that looked like an ash tray. I pitched my tissue in the receptacle and as it entered it splashed. Holy Water! We applied the rule given to drivers hauling trash from a construction site – Don't Look Back. My daughter has a sense of humor like mine, and we were both staggering along laughing and receiving questioning looks from everyone around us.

We can't go back to that church.

MARK MOWER

A good friend of mine, Mark, has volunteered a story from his past to be included in this book. Mark is a very technical person and problem solver, having been a welder, plumbing contractor, owning a company building booster pumps, doing commercial piping, and several more. He was born in Daytona Beach but when he was five years old his parents divorced, and he moved to Adel, Georgia, to live with his grandmother. Granny had a large yard of around five and a half acres that trailed out to some trees and a swampy area. An older fellow with a heavy limp would regularly mow the yard with a hand mower. While mowing one day and all the way to the back of the property, the mower caught on fire. The mower was sitting there in flames and still running while the poor guy went limping back to the house for something to put out the fire. Mark was about eight years old at the time and began using his analytical mind to solve the problem. The solution was to pee on the mower and seemed to be solving the problem until one technical detail surfaced. When peeing on the spark plug, a few thousand volts came instantly back up the stream with an extremely painful shock to a personal area. Upon returning with the water to put out the fire, the yard man found Mark rolling in the grass in extreme pain.

Please don't try this at home, as there is a 100% chance of extreme pain.

REX

Rex was the name chosen by a friend for his Rhodesian Ridgeback puppy. Actually, Rex is short for Tyrannosaurus Rex. Ridgebacks were bred in Rhodesia, now Zimbabwe, to protect the household because they would back down lions. They are known there as lion hounds and could hold a lion at bay until his master would arrive to kill the lion. Why would anyone want a Pitbull when they could have a Ridgeback? Rex grew to one hundred twenty pounds and was quite large. In the animal world, Rex was am equivalent to Albert Einstein, and probably the smartest dog I've seen. While a puppy, Mark (his owner) went out to get his morning paper. After the second day, Rex would race ahead, pick up the paper, and return to the house. He would also race out to the mail carrier and stand on his hind legs by the mail truck looking at the driver eyeball to eyeball, barking for the mail so he could take it in. Mail carriers new to the route from time to time were scared to death.

He was a friendly dog, especially to people he liked. If he liked you, he would walk around you howling, rubbing and walking between your legs as you entered the house. This was a problem for short people.

Mark took him to obedience training when he was about half grown, and was told that trying to train a Ridgeback was a waste of time as they were too stubborn. Mark had confidence in Rex and took him to training, disregarding the instructor's opinion. An obedience test in the class required the dog to sit while the owner walked about thirty yards away. The dog would then be given a signal to come to the master. Rex took off like a race horse and when halfway was given the signal to stop. At that point he hit the dirt and slid about five feet. Rex was given the award as the smartest dog and the most obedient there.

One evening Mark and his wife, Julie, had a few people over for steamed oysters. Mark and I were steaming the oysters in the back yard and applying hot sauce and horse radish. Everybody ate their fill, and Mark and I were still eating and having adult beverages. Of course Rex was with us, he was one of the guys. He could look at you with the saddest brown eyes as he always wanted whatever we were eating. The adult beverages were partially responsible for the decision to include Rex in the feast. After eating his first oyster, Rex came back for more. I don't really know how many he ate, but we couldn't refuse him as it was male bonding time. The next day when returning to the house they discovered that Rex didn't do so well with the oysters, hot sauce and horse radish. Rex had shit from one end of the house to the other and even on the walls.

Oysters with hot sauce and horseradish were not a good thing to feed the dog. Julie did, however, get all new carpet and fresh paint.

CARPAL TUNNEL SYNDROME

My wife had carpal tunnel syndrome in her right hand, and the occasional numbness and pain were getting worse. At night she wore a brace for some relief, but that was doing little to correct the situation. The strength in the hand was decreasing and it became difficult to lift items like a milk jug or laundry soap bottle. A couple of her friends had the carpal tunnel surgery with success. They encouraged her to do the same, so she made the decision to have it done.

We began the process of looking for a local surgeon to perform the operation. On the internet we found what appeared to be two good local doctors. In order to select the right one we started reading the reviews of previous patients. The reviews would generally start with a rating of the office staff in promptness, efficiency and attitude. Next was the wait time for the doctor after arrival for an appointment or time from arrival until being seen by the doctor. After that, the attentiveness of the doctor and the amount of time spent before moving on to the next patient.

In reading the reviews, I could see her keen interest in what each person reported. I read some of the reviews aloud so we could both know the content. When coming to the end of the last review I continued as if still reading with an additional comment as follows:

I noticed as I was coming out from under the sedation that my pants were unzipped and my ass was sore.

She turned and gave me the most horrified look, but when she saw me laughing she realized the last sentence was bogus.

LET'S DO SOMETHING NEW!!

Have you ever read a book of guy stories? Well, I haven't either. Now that does not say that none exist, it just says I'm not aware of any. What is a guy story? The type of story that is told when a few guys or girls get together and start talking about their day or something they experienced. Also, stories they have been told. These stories may or may not be funny but are worth telling. An example of a guy story is as follows.

In that period of life between graduation from school and marriage when you can choose how you spend your time and money, a group of guys in my town formed a hot rod club. We elected officers, took up dues and rented a garage capable of housing around eight cars. We proceeded to build cars, mostly Model A Fords, with big engines. We cut up and modified more Model A's than Henry Ford could build in a week. The aging process of marriage and jobs picked us off one by one ending the club, but one fellow stayed with the effort. He began building and racing dragsters. He used Chrysler Hemi engines and became very successful. He continued to live in WV and would drive to Texas, Illinois, and Michigan over the weekend. One weekend in Detroit he was staging for a race when the guy that started each race asked him to do something that would give him a disadvantage in the race. A heated argument with yelling and arm waving ensued. He saw about ten guys jump the fence and start running toward the argument. Our guy, when seeing this group running toward him, became quite worried. It turns out they were all from WV coming to his defense. It pays to be a country boy!

I'm asking for stories from you to be included in a book of Guy Stories. Your name may or may not be included as well as your town or location. It is up to you. Whether the story is true or not makes no difference. Email stories to tomodaniel39@gmail.com.

How about stories from your military experience? Here is one from mine.

In the Army I was stationed at Fort Knox for a short time for training. One day I was seated at a table with four other guys in the PX. At that time, I weighed around 190 pounds. I mention this because the guys at my table made me look like a midget. The largest weighed 305 and the smallest around 260. The one weighing 305 had grown up on Tyler Mountain,

WV, working at his dad's junk yard. He was not fat and was about the strongest man I ever knew. One of the guys was nicknamed "goof", which you did not call him to his face as he was around 6'5". He didn't like the nickname and let one fellow who called him that regret his mistake. A group of six or seven young soldiers walked up to our table. They all appeared to be just out of high school and no older than eighteen. Nobody in the group weighed over 170 pounds. They had just graduated from airborne school. The instructors there had done an excellent job with these men, as they all knew they could whip Superman with one hand tied behind them. Their boots were bloused as were ours because we were Armor. Bloused boots are when the pants cuff is tucked into the top of your boots. The guys in front mentioned that our boots were bloused like theirs and if we did not pull our pants cuffs out, they would cut them off. Buck, at 6'5" and 305 pounds, stood up and told them, "You boys don't want to cut off anything you can't eat." They looked up at Buck and then wandered off.

Lightning Source UK Ltd.
Milton Keynes UK
UKHW041930150822
407355UK00003B/63

9 781480 892002